"Jordan Paul has spent most of his adult life considering the interplay of heart, soul, spirit, and mystery. Now, he uses his wisdom and insight to lead readers on a compelling journey whose destination holds the promise of a life of personal and spiritual growth. But be aware that Jordan goes well beyond the inspirational to provide specific information and guidance you can use immediately. Think of this book as a guidebook for the rest of your life."

–JAMES A. AUTRY, author of *The Servant Leader* and *The Spirit of Retirement* (Fall, 2002)

"With a unique synthesis of teaching stories and practical wisdom, Dr. Paul helps people move out of the darkness of blame and conflict avoidance and into the light of personal empowerment, constructive engagement, and enduring intimacy."

–DENNIS JAFFE, Ph.D., author of *Take This Job and Love It* and *Working with the Ones You Love*

"*Becoming Your Own Hero* reflects the essence of Unity's teaching. Jordan's spiritual insights, combined with his practical wisdom, not only inspire, but also remind us always that it is the heart connection that ultimately matters."

–ROSEMARY FILLMORE RHEA, consultant, Unity School of Christianity, author of *How My Spirit Travels* (2003)

"Dr. Jordan Paul is a grand master of Positive Insight and just keeps getting better with every book. *Becoming Your Own Hero* is a celebration of one of life's greatest adventures, improving your relationship with yourself and everyone in your world and letting the way of your heart be the heart of your way."

–DR. JAY SCOTT NEALE, RScD, Pastor and Director, Tri City Church of Religious Science, Center for Positive Living, Fremont, California

Becoming Your Own Hero

Jordan Paul, Ph.D.

HARA
PUBLISHING GROUP

Published By
Hara Publishing
P.O. Box 19732
Seattle, WA 98109

Copyright ©2003 by
Dr. Jordan Paul
All rights reserved

ISBN: 0-9710724-9-3

Library of Congress Catalog Card Number:
2002116821

Manufactured in the United States
10 9 8 7 6 5 4 3 2

Editor: Vicki McCown
Cover Design: Robilyn Robbins
Book Design: Stephanie Martindale
Back Cover Photo of Jordan Paul: Linda Compton
Cover Photo: Mark Tomalty - Masterfile

Contents

Acknowledgments

In each day of my life there are moments when I stop and feel deep gratitude for the many people and events that have been a necessary part of bringing me to this point in my life. Singling out specific people is not meant to discount the importance of others, but I especially want to thank:

My entire family, who supported me through a journey that took much longer than anyone expected; especially **Bob**, for your enormous heart and incredible wisdom; **Mom** for your unwavering optimism; and **Dad**, who even though you aren't here to see the finished product are a major reason for its completion.

Lee Shapiro for being my rock, always there in any way that I need you. Whether you are exploring ideas or plumbing the depths of inner space, your insights are forever etched in me.

Bill Kaufman for pushing me to "say it simply, clearly, and with examples." What a joy you are in my life.

Jeff Kasmar for painstakingly reading and correcting version, after version, after version, and for being a pretty darn good dance teacher as well.

Marla Wilson, Printed Page Productions, for paying attention to the details while opening up new ways to see the creative process.

"What I want to describe to you next," said Varela, "is in the spiritual realm—spiritual because it has to do with human hearts. When we are in touch with our 'open nature,' our emptiness, we exert an enormous attraction to other human beings. There is great magnetism in that state of being which has been called by Trungpa (Rimpoche) 'authentic presence.'" Varela leaned back and smiled. *"Isn't that beautiful? And if others are in that same space or entering it, they resonate with us and immediately doors are open to us. It is not strange or mystical. It is part of the natural order.*

"Those that are in touch with that capacity are seen as great warriors in the American Indian tradition, or as Samurai in the Eastern tradition. For me, the Samurai is one who holds that posture in the world—someone who is so open he is ready to die for the cause. That capacity gives us a fundamental key and is a state of being known in all great traditions of humanity."

Later in the conversation, Varela warned, "There is great danger if we consider these people to be exceptional. They are not. This capacity is a part of the natural order and is a manifestation of something we haven't seen previously, not something we do not have. This state is available to us all, and yet it is the greatest of all human treasures.

"This state—where we connect deeply with others and doors open—is there waiting for us. It is like an optical illusion. All we have to do is squint and see that it has been there all along, waiting for us. All we have to do is to see the oneness that we are."

Part of a conversation between Joseph Jaworski and Francisco Varela as told by Jaworski in his book, *Synchronicity: The Inner Path of Leadership*, Joseph Jaworski, Berrett-Koehler, San Francisco, 1996.

Chapter One

The Heart of a Hero

Even the most exalted states and the most exceptional spiritual accomplishments are unimportant if we cannot be happy in the most basic and ordinary ways, if we cannot touch one another and the life we have been given with our hearts.
—Jack Kornfield, Ph.D., *A Path with Heart*

In a past life as a psychotherapist, teacher, writer, and seminar leader, I achieved everything I believed would make me happy. I had a beautiful and fascinating wife, a wonderful family, a handsome home, and wealth beyond my wildest expectations. I also had coauthored a best-selling book and was a highly paid motivational speaker who traveled the country presenting seminars and serving as a regular guest on talk shows. To the outside world I probably seemed successful and powerful. Inside, however, was a gnawing omnipresent low-level anxiety and discontent. I had no intimate friendships and I was becoming more and more irritable and unhappy. Then, my marriage began to unravel. And, so did I.

Well-meaning friends tried to reassure me with variations on the theme of "You just need to see this as an opportunity." But, framed in self-doubt, the echo of words I had once spoken to reassure others only left me irritated and frustrated. Under the looming specter of being alone, I came face to face with not only the insecurities that led to my unhappiness, but with the belief that created my most terrifying fear: Without a strong and competent woman I could not be happy or successful.

At that time, I had no clue that my journey would lead to parts of myself I had never known and to a greater sense of personal power and contentment than I ever dreamed possible. I only had a vague awareness that

1

even though I was a well-respected member of my community, I felt like a fraud and was terrified of being found out and ending up alone.

My new life began with the realization that what kept me feeling weak and insecure was my dependency upon people and things for my sense of well-being. I dedicated myself to confronting that dependency, and vowed to not appear as a public speaker until I had healed those wounds. I gave myself five years to accomplish that task. At the time I naïvely believed I could control the future simply through the energy of my own thoughts. It has been fourteen years. Humility was then, and remains, one of my major lessons.

During my journey I have met many people, both personally and through books and films, who have shown me the way to find greater fulfillment in both my personal relationships and work. By inspiring me to rise above commonplace behavior and live in integrity with the best that is within me, they are my heroes.

I discovered one such hero, St. Francis of Assisi, in the film, *Brother Sun Sister Moon*. The scene that particularly struck me was when Francis renounces the life of wealth and privilege into which he had been born and proclaims, "I want to be happy. I want to live like the birds in the sky. I want to experience the freedom and the purity that they experience. The rest is of no use to me. If the purpose of life is this loveless toil we fill our days with, then it is not for me. There must be something better. There has to be. Man is a spirit, he has a soul. That is what I want to recapture, my soul. I want to live. I want to live in the fields. Stride over hills. Climb trees. Swim rivers. I want to feel the firm grasp of the earth beneath my feet, without shoes, without possessions, without those shadows we call our servants."

My heroes demonstrate the courage to live congruently with their true selves. To live with that kind of integrity, and thus become our own heroes, we must connect with who we really are.

Watching *Brother Sun Sister Moon* was one of many experiences that helped me connect to the essence of myself, my soul, my heart. Learning to find my heart and recapture my soul has allowed more of the sacred connections that have created greater harmony and balance, pierced the veil of my separateness, and made me more complete. Heart connections have given all other things meaning.

When connected to my heart, I can connect in satisfying ways to others and to the mystery that is beyond humanness, which may be thought of as God, nature, and/or Spirit. The more time I connect in this way, the more I feel fulfilled and like my own hero.

The importance of connectinting to one's heart is traditional wisdom, transcending any single religion and common to all. It has opened me to a wide diversity of sources to help me connect more to my heart. While today the heart is associated with feelings or love, in ancient times the heart was associated with the very totality of the human psyche. The Bible contains many references to the heart. In Mark 8:17, a hard heart is associated with not hearing, not seeing, not understanding, and not remembering. In Isaiah 63:17, "...a hard heart does not know the sacred and has no sense of awe." Understanding the heart as our essence means that it influences every aspect of our lives, our feeling, thinking, willing, and seeing. It is the heart of the matter.

Everything that is satisfying flows naturally from an open heart. Such experiences and feelings include compassion, joy, forgiveness, faith, an openness to learning, a sense of meaning, freedom, contentment, self-worth, and ecstasy. With an open heart, we are fully present in the moment and our bodies are liberated from anxiety. It feels like coming home, and it is magical.

Reflect upon your own life and recall times when you have felt the magnificence and satisfaction of an open heart. You may have been dancing, listening to music, touched emotionally during a film, or watching a sunset.

Openhearted engagement with others allows more magic to happen. A loving connection satisfies the deep and rarely met need to be seen, understood, valued, and appreciated. This may have occurred while looking into your baby's eyes, while engaged in lovemaking, or even perhaps during a brief conversation with a stranger.

Since we disconnect from our hearts only when we are afraid, the issue on which my journey has focused, and which I believe to be at the core of the unhappiness for most of us, is the fear of losing, or not having enough of, something we believe we need for our sense of well-being. For example, we might think we need a relationship, a sexual experience, money, a substance (alcohol, drugs), a different body type, to change our feelings or behavior, or to obtain the approval of others.

That dependency is the weakness that keeps us from being truly powerful. It is our Achilles' heel. Even when we seem powerful to the outside world, whatever we fear losing is our shadow—the chink in our armor that we desperately try to hide. Whenever that fear is activated we will do anything to avoid facing it, including compromising our own integrity as well as the integrity of others.

We are then caught in life's most vicious circle. Attempts to protect ourselves from losing what we think we need results in the erosion of our self-respect, the one thing we truly need to feel whole and fulfilled. This results in greater insecurities and the need to protect ourselves, which results in the erosion of our self-respect, and so on. Since we can never get enough of that which we do not really need, we are stuck. Only getting what we truly need fulfills us.

At those times when we are not needy we can stand squarely in who we really are. We feel proud of ourselves. That is true personal power. When we are afraid, we compromise ourselves, and that leaves us feeling weak and insecure. Staying connected to our essence happens only when we know that, even should we lose something, we will not just survive but will thrive. Therefore, staying in integrity can occur only when we are not afraid of loss, whether that loss is a relationship, material things, or even our lives.

Although we attempt to hide our dependency and fear of loss from others and ourselves, our behavior speaks volumes. The juxtaposition of dependency and real power is evidenced in every area of life. For example, as a nation, our Achilles' heel is our dependency on oil to maintain our economy or lifestyle. The fear of losing the resource we believe we cannot live without can bring the most powerful nation in the world to its knees by compromising our integrity to maintain alliances and policies that are not in our best interest.

As individuals we compromise our integrity when we believe that we need:

- Another person's approval, and then manipulate ourselves into being what they want us to be
- To be in a relationship with another person, and then attempt to maintain control over him or her
- More things or money to feel content, and then sacrifice our relationship with ourselves and others while on a never-ending, and often escalating, treadmill of discontent
- To change our physical appearance to be happy with how we look, and then spend inordinate amounts of time and money attempting to hide what we cannot accept
- To change our feelings or behavior, and thus have judged ourselves as bad or wrong
- Sex to feel okay or be happy, and then manipulatively attempt to get what we want

Since true power does not fear loss, it does not need to control. When we do not have to manipulate and control others to have power over them or to control the future, we can stay in integrity no matter what happens. We can be content with who we are and with what we have. That acceptance propels us forward into fulfilling more of our potential and becoming more of our own hero.

The ability to stay connected to our hearts, especially in the face of difficulties, is the greatest challenge in becoming truly powerful. Simply put, "Who is powerful? People who close their hearts and strike back out of fear that they will lose something or those who stay in integrity by maintaining their openness?" The oft-quoted idea from Rudyard Kipling's poem *If* challenges us to keep our head when all about us are losing theirs. Substituting "heart" for "head" and therefore keeping our heart when all about us are losing theirs, is the power I'm talking about.

Heart power is a core teaching of our most inspirational heros, such as Jesus, Gandhi, and Martin Luther King. They each applied the principles of love and respect to creating transformational political reform. They did not, however, provide many models for applying their principles to close interpersonal relationships. This book addresses that challenge.

The thought that personal fulfillment comes from being connected to one's heart may seem obvious, but I am appalled by how almost all of what I was taught led me to distrust my heart and my ability to connect to it. Instead, I adopted beliefs that sentenced me to a lifetime of living without the faith that I could create my own sense of well-being. In trying to avoid my dreaded demons of rejection and loneliness, I became slavishly hooked into pursuing things which I hoped would ease my anxiety, such as women, sex, money, success, other people's approval, love, material things, clothes, and expensive cars.

I did not know that it was a disconnection from my heart that kept me insecure and dependent. I did not know that being imprisoned by the fear of my inability to create my own sense of well-being created a need for control that pushed away the connection for which I did not even consciously know I yearned. When I realized that connection to my heart creates the love that every wise person knows will bring contentment, my sentence of living without faith was commuted.

Each time I think about my previous life, I am touched with sorrow at the many missed opportunities for wonderful connections with ex-wives, children, friends, and clients. I feel this pain without guilt or recrimination because I know that my inability to open my heart is never because I am bad, wrong, or inadequate. I am, like everyone else, always doing the best I can and it is only a lack of information and fear that creates my difficulties. Still, I feel sadness at the thought of people trying to get their basic need for connection met and instead creating separation and alienation because of fear and ignorance.

Fulfilling Connections and Heart Feelings

Fulfillment results when an open heart is integral to an activity. Each of us has many natural abilities, such as to feel, learn, and play. An ability itself, however, can result in a Fulfilling Connection only when it is empowered by the feelings that come from the heart. For example, heartfelt touch creates a Fulfilling Connection during times of distress, a sexual experience, or while being massaged. When the heart is not present, touching another creates separation, alienation, and dissatisfaction.

An open heart produces:
- Touch that is soothing and giving
- Play that is rejuvenating and joyful
- Productivity that is exciting and satisfying
- Learning that is meaningful and exhilarating

Disconnection from heart produces:
- Touch that is unpleasant and demanding
- Play that is aggressive and tense
- Productivity that is tedious and unsatisfying
- Learning that is meaningless and boring

To realize the power of the heart to create Fulfilling Connections you have only to consider the times when an open heart has been present and contrast them with the times when it has been absent. To determine if an open heart is active during any activity, ask yourself:

- Am I being touched emotionally or physically in a way that feels healing?
- Is something of value being created, given, or received?
- Is there an openness to learning?
- Am I feeling relaxed and fulfilled?

If the answer to any of the above questions is "No," an open heart is not present and Fulfilling Connections are not happening.

Although the ability to feel is natural, feelings do not always come from an open heart. Heartfelt feelings are warm, tender, mellow, and caring. However, their expression in tears, laughter, and in acts of caring can also leave us vulnerable to the sting of criticism from others—as well as from ourselves. Cold, harsh, and uncaring feelings such as anger, greed, blame, depression, arrogance, hatred, disdain, and jealousy reflect a disconnection from heart.

When fears block Heart Feelings, it does not mean we are bad or unloving, or that we do not love ourselves or others. It only means that fear is reigning, Heart Feelings are silent, and our behavior is not loving at that moment. Similarly, when Heart Feelings predominate, it does not mean that our fears are not there, only that they are not getting in the way of our Heart Feelings. In any given moment, fears can be activated and overpower Heart Feelings—and vice versa.

Fulfilling Connections occur, therefore, from moment to moment. By learning from those times when Heart Feelings are blocked, moments of Fulfilling Connection can be extended in time and circumstance.

Compassion and joy are the two seminal Heart Feelings. Compassion is a powerful idea central to all major religions. It has commonly been defined as "to suffer with." But as Marcus Borg, Hundere Distinguished Professor of Religion and Culture at Oregon State University, points out in *Meeting Jesus Again for the First Time*, "In terms of feeling, compassion means 'to feel with' as even the etymology of the English word suggests: passion comes from the Latin word that means 'to feel,' and the prefix com- means 'with.' Compassion thus means feeling the feelings and situation of another in a visceral way, at a level somewhere below the level of the head."

In this book, compassion is meant as feeling empathy toward oneself and others in all feeling states, not just in suffering. Compassion is feeling the sorrow of a friend who has lost a loved one, certainly, but it is more than that. Compassion is feeling the:

- fear in a fellow committee member who is raising his or her voice in anger at you
- joy in your partner who has healed a rift with a friend you may not personally like
- sadness you feel when you have made a serious mistake in your work
- upset in an employee who is behaving obnoxiously toward you

- disappointment and fear in your teenage child who comes home with a bad report card, or your pain when she tells you she is pregnant

Compassion produces the feelings and behavior that create openhearted engagement with others, to the spiritual life, and to our essence. In fact, Borg states in *Meeting Jesus Again for the First Time*, "For Jesus, compassion was the central quality of God and the central moral quality of a life centered in God. The crystallization of Jesus' message, 'Be compassionate as God is compassionate,' speaks of a way of life grounded in an imitatio dei, an imitation of God. To be compassionate is what is meant elsewhere in the New Testament by the somewhat more abstract command 'to love.'"

When connected to our compassion, the sacred within us is illuminated and it is impossible to run roughshod over the sacred that lies within others. With compassion informing our behavior, love and caring toward others and ourselves flow naturally. At those times, play cannot be a win/lose contest; touch cannot be inappropriately sexual or harmful; productivity cannot mistreat others or the environment; feelings cannot be criticized and repressed; and learning cannot be blocked.

Joy expresses the love in what you are doing. When you are not self-conscious and worried about being judged, you just "flow" and life is fun. The Jesuit mystic and archeologist Teilhard de Chardin said, "Joy is the only true sign of the presence of God."

Feeling joy requires not taking things so seriously. What if life is not intended to be such a serious affair? Think back to the countless number of times you became upset with something—being late, a spilled glass of milk, a lover's rejection, a disappointment of expectations, how you looked physically—only to think sometime later, "Why did I make such a big deal over that? It doesn't seem very important right now." Remembering "the reason angels can fly is because they take themselves lightly" may help give a lighter perspective to your life.

Not taking things so seriously also allows experiencing a great deal more from every situation. Matthew Fox, founder and president of the University of Creation Spirituality, said in *The Coming of the Cosmic Christ*, "In allowing one's authentic awe and wonder to be born again and in welcoming the puer, the child and playfulness, to come to self-expression, one is already involved in co-creation. For there is no creation without play. The Cosmic Christ is a comic Christ with a sense of humor."

Maintaining a sense of humor requires seeing the lighter side of things and living as the Buddhist saying advises, "Act always as if the future of the Universe depended on what you did, while laughing at yourself for thinking that whatever you do makes any difference." Nurturing your ability to feel joy may require challenging the beliefs that have created inhibiting fears. The Fulfillment Connections Process described in the appendix is designed to help release those inhibitions.

Expressing Heart Feelings

Heart Feelings find their natural expressions in tears, laughter, contentment, acceptance, faith, and forgiveness. These behaviors forge an openhearted engagement with oneself and open the door for deep and meaningful connections with others. When unfettered by fear, expressions of Heart Feelings are full and passionate. Laughter is not stuck in the throat, sadness is not repressed behind the eyes, and orgasm is not restricted to the genitals. Each expression becomes a childlike (not childish) outpouring of feeling that consumes the entire body while both bathing and cleansing us. Such a free expression of feeling opens us to simultaneously giving and receiving love.

Tears are a natural release of Heart Feelings. In addition to expressing pain, they often accompany joy and awe. When fear does not hold them back, tears flow easily and we feel peaceful.

I was almost forty years old before I discovered the joy of crying. I had always tried to hold back my tears. I often wanted to cry during movies, but by clenching my face, or deflecting my thoughts, I fought my tears. Most of the time I was successful, but I would walk out of the theater with a pounding at the back of my neck and a head that felt twice its size. If I was with another person, I held myself together by walking briskly and avoiding eye contact or conversation.

Slowly, I began to realize that by repressing my feelings I was denying my true self and distancing myself from others. I began the process of freeing the sensitive part of myself. It's been a gradual process, but now I can openly weep, and I love it. I'm proud that I can be touched emotionally and am not afraid to show that part of myself. When I am with a person whom I care deeply about, we hold each other, experiencing together the comfort and delicious intimacy of shared Heart Feelings. Giving myself permission to cry not only makes me feel more powerful; it allows a deeper level of emotional intimacy with both women and men.

Laughter is the natural expression of joy. Most of us know the difference between a laugh emanating from a constricted throat and a belly laugh that comes from the entire body. Unleashing the genie of laughter is an unforgettable, full-body experience that leaves us spent and satisfied, as well as creating Fulfilling Connections with others. By reducing tension and releasing bodily energy, laughter speeds healing and helps keep us in good physical shape. Muted joy has no memorable physical or emotional effects.

Acceptance of situations and behaviors follows from compassion. Feeling deeply into a situation averts any critical judgment, or a desire to change anything. We naturally accept that people and situations are exactly as they must be. For example, we embrace a person terrified of being alone and remaining in an abusive relationship, or people with an overwhelming fear of losing their image or identity that keeps them from committing to an intimate relationship. Whenever compassionate acceptance is lost, learning the very important reasons that situations are as they are reconnects us to Heart Feelings and to acceptance.

Faith and acceptance are soul mates and with them comes contentment. Faith lies in knowing that no matter what life gives us, we will survive. The more we realize that we can survive anything, including failures, abandonment, betrayal, disasters, and even death, the more faith we will have, and the less need we will feel for control over the future actions of people and events.

A deeper level of faith requires more than just knowing we will survive. It means believing in our ability to thrive—to pick ourselves up, learn from the experience, and emerge better off than we were before. It is the faith that connection to our hearts will result in the behavior that leads to getting what we truly desire.

When fear gives way to faith, we can allow room for both ourselves and others to be our unique selves. As faith grows, our ability to let go of control and live in harmony with life increases. By not having our behavior dictated by fear, we feel more powerful and we thrive. The greater our fears, the less faith we have. Developing greater faith, which involves understanding, confronting, and testing out our fears, is illustrated in the following two chapters.

Forgiveness as a natural extension of compassion differs significantly from traditional ideas about forgiveness. Traditional concepts of forgiveness, which can occur without compassion, allow behavior to be categorized into right and wrong boxes. That kind of forgiveness is merely a pardoning of transgressions. Waving the wand of absolution is condescending and alienating, and it locks the forgiver into feelings of self-righteousness and blame.

Holding a grudge or being defensive and angry binds us to those very feelings and judgments. Alienated from Heart Feelings, we cannot forgive ourselves, and therefore we can neither receive forgiveness nor forgive others. Traditional forgiveness does not help overcome this alienation and is therefore not nurturing to others or ourselves.

Compassionate forgiveness, however, understands that, given our fears and ignorance, we and others are always doing the best we can, and that we are neither wrong nor bad. In reality, there is nothing to forgive; there is only acceptance. Acceptance does not condone behavior. It does not mean that some actions are not harmful and that we need to protect ourselves from predators. It does not take away our sadness over what we missed due to our own fears and disconnected behaviors, or the fear or behavior of others.

When we are truly accepting, we know that things in the past could not have been any different, and thus forgiveness occurs naturally. Acceptance allows us to forgive ourselves, and that is where true healing begins. Compassionate forgiveness enables us to feel better about ourselves and to have more experiences that leave us feeling really powerful.

If you find it difficult to practice compassionate forgiveness, you can begin moving toward Fulfilling Connections by first making it acceptable that you are not able to do it. Then you can learn what is blocking your compassionate forgiveness.

For example, you may discover the fear that if you feel compassion, you will be more vulnerable to being taken advantage of. If this is the case, see if you can respect the fact that until you have more confidence in your ability to set boundaries, your self-protecting behavior is necessary. If you can give yourself this acceptance, you will feel content and more ready to take the next step, which might entail understanding more about what it means to set boundaries without losing your compassion. If you cannot respect your self-protectiveness, you can learn what is blocking that acceptance.

The Sound of One Heart Opening

People who have a strong connection to their Heart Feelings distinguish themselves because of the powerful effect they have on others. Although you have no control over whether or when others will open their hearts with you, opening your heart allows others the opportunity to be open and to experience a magical sense of oneness.

The following event was chronicled by a police officer in a small town in Colorado.

I pulled up behind a car stopped in the middle of the street. Turning on my flashing lights, I motioned to the driver to move to the side of the road. She followed my directions, but as she did she gave me the finger.

Anger boiled up in me and, armed with self-righteousness, I decided to teach her a lesson in manners and slap her with a hefty ticket. I got out of my car and as I approached her car I pulled myself up to my full intimidating height. Noting how rigidly she was holding herself, I approached with caution.

As she rolled down the window, I sensed sadness behind her bristling armor. My anger drained away and I found myself feeling compassion and saying, "You must be having a really difficult day." At that, her tension dissolved, her eyes filled with tears, and she began to recount the painful events she had just been through. Her pain touched me. I'd heard enough stories by people trying to con me to know that this one was sincere.

Before we went our separate ways we spent a few minutes sharing some thoughts and feelings about life's difficulties. We also shared how wonderful our interaction had left us feeling.

By connecting with his Heart Feelings, the policeman experienced Fulfilling Connections with himself and with her. In those few moments he was his own hero. He reported feeling more meaning in his life than he had ever felt before, and he wanted more of it. In fact, he said, "For the first time I knew what my chief meant when he told us that we were not police officers, we were peace officers."

The Heart of Service

The loving behavior that naturally flows from Heart Feelings makes any activity an opportunity to be of service, whether at home, at work or in nature. It is therefore an integral part of the journey toward becoming your own hero. Although many activities begin with Heart Feelings being active, hearts routinely close behind other seeming priorities and being of service often becomes lost. When hearts close:

- Getting a spouse and/or children to do what we want becomes more important than meeting their needs
- Making a point becomes more important than really hearing another
- Making a profit becomes more important than caring about the lives of clients and employees or about the well-being of our environment
- Maintaining power becomes more important than empowering others
- Giving information becomes more important than teaching students to love learning
- Winning takes precedence over the self-esteem of athletes

An openness to learning about being of service is an essential part of the journey. Some of questions that illuminate this quest are the focus of this book: What does it mean to be of service to yourself? What does it mean to be of service to others? What does it mean to be of service to others and not lose yourself in the process?

When a heart is open, the experience of giving back is fulfilling. For example, mentoring is an extraordinarily powerful activity gaining in popularity. It affords an incredible opportunity to teach about Fulfilling Connections. Unfortunately, most mentoring programs emphasize only the passing on of job skills. Although this is very valuable, it remains incomplete.

Imagine the mentor being an elder, passing on skills for living a more fulfilling life. To pass on such wisdom, mentors would have to have transcended their own cultural biases and the limitations on the expression of their own Heart Feelings. With a primary motivation of teaching about fulfillment, mentors would instead create an environment where participants could get to know each other more deeply. They would facilitate learning more about the way they and others feel and think. They would experience learning that appreciates and respects the differences and similarities in others.

Training mentors to access their Heart Feelings and then passing them on to their mentees would give the mentoring experience a richness that would greatly increase the benefit for both mentor and mentee, as well as for our entire society.

Creating Space for Fulfilling Connections

Fulfilling Connections do not usually happen instantaneously. It's hard to imagine two stressed people, after a long work day, meeting the needs of their kids and the demands of their household, turning out the lights, and then immediately falling into connecting to their own hearts and to each other heart to heart. The only place they are likely to fall is into an exhausted sleep.

The complexity and demands of today's lifestyle make Fulfilling Connections more and more difficult to attain. Our current mania for accumulating things shrinks the space that encourages Fulfilling Connections.

That space, which comes from a slower pace that allows for wandering and wondering, used to exist naturally within extended families, small towns, neighborhoods, and schools. It is in the free-flowing time of just hanging out together that the magic of openhearted engagement often happens. Long, slow dinners, walks in the park, and even doing chores together allowed space and time for Heart Feelings to be integrated into the important concerns and questions that surface in relaxed human interactions.

Today that kind of space has become nearly extinct, giving way to overstressed and overworked parents, grandparents who live too far away to be regularly available, unknown neighbors, and speedy transportation that whisks us past each other, as well as past any natural beauty that may have survived our "advancing civilization." In addition, the computer and Internet, which allow communication to take place without ever having to meet face to face and heart to heart, threaten to complete our headlong rush into isolation and alienation. Even when parents make great efforts to spend quality time with their children, the demands of professional careers, earning enough money to insure a quality life for their children, and attending to their own personal needs make unstructured time a rare commodity.

I have come to greatly appreciate the importance of living simply. In giving up a lifestyle in which I accumulated many wonderful things, I have substituted the freedom of not having to support those things. I do not have to work long hours and have learned to live "simply rich."

In an economy that is based on creating beliefs that our unhappiness is because we don't have enough of something, that may seem downright un-American. I don't own a big house, a late-model car, lots of clothes and jewelry, go out to fancy restaurants, or indulge in expensive entertainment or recreational activities. I do have time to connect with nature, my friends, and myself while walking and allowing conversations to wind into deep and wonderful places.

Although many of us are familiar with the moments of Fulfilling Connections that occur after a fight when we are making up, that's not a very appealing way to attain them. Simplicity creates the possibility for Fulfilling Connections to occur in pleasant ways.

In the following anecdote, my daughter Sheryl explains how the space for openhearted engagement allowed Fulfilling Connections to develop within herself and between herself and her grandparents:

> Upon graduating from college, I realized that although my intellectual and creative parts were well developed, I knew very little about my domestic side. I had grown up in a typical upper-middle class American family with two working parents who had very demanding careers and domestic help who handled all household chores.
>
> To learn more about the domestic side of myself, I decided to live for a year in an apartment below my grandparents' home. Grandpa Izzy became my earth mentor. I worked with him tending the twenty fruit trees and rows and rows of flowers and vegetables in his quarter-acre organic garden. And, to learn about homemaking, I apprenticed with Grandma Charlotte.
>
> During that year, I learned much more than how to garden and how to prepare healthy and delicious meals. As Grandma and I made dinner each evening, our conversations flowed freely. We not only talked about the wealth of food ideas she had gathered over fifty years of cooking, but a wide range of subjects—including our personal thoughts and feelings.

Beginning the Journey

I offer the information in this book with a strong belief that there is not a single or exclusive path to wisdom, that there are no easy answers, and that my truth is not "the truth." Since easy answers are usually attempts to try to have control rather than truly empower us to have faith in ourselves and in life itself, there are no prescribed simplistic solutions. How a particular person reached the awareness that helped create a new life is not important. In fact, learning about another person's path is often counterproductive when people decide to emulate that person. Instead, to help you find your unique path, stories and anecdotes are included here that illustrate people finding wisdom in many different ways.

Although this book presents information that is new for me, it does not mean that there is anything new in it. Real wisdom is timeless and universal. It is the basis of many spiritual and religious disciplines. It lies within each of us. Included here are the valuable lessons I have learned. I have gained this information not because I am any smarter or more spiritually evolved than you are, but because the circumstances of my life opened them to me. The only thing new is the way the material is presented. I am hoping it will help you access and utilize what, on some level, you already know.

But I do offer the following Satisfaction Guarantee for the information you gain from this book.

SATISFACTION GUARANTEE

When connected to your heart, you will feel satisfied by the fulfillment that comes from

BEING YOUR OWN HERO

As in accomplishing anything worthwhile, fully understanding and integrating this information will be challenging. Discovering personal and universal truths and thus living in harmony with one's essence is fraught with obstacles and detours. Learning to manage the frustrations that accompany any unrealistic expectations about this journey being quick and effortless or ending in a predetermined outcome is an important place to begin. For me, life is all about the journey. My journey continues to be refreshing, exciting, and fulfilling. I am honored that you are allowing me to be part of your journey.

Chapter Two

Heart Learning

When your heart speaks, take good notes.

—Anonymous

Allowing innate curiosity to drive a desire to learn more about Heart Feelings is how you learn to be your own hero. This is Heart Learning and it is how Fulfilling Connections can be experienced more of the time.

Sometimes, in the flow of an activity, Heart Learning occurs without our awareness. Learning about love at the beginning of a relationship is such an instance. When you fall in love, you don't analyze what's happening. Not limited by your self-protections, the transformative power of love sweeps you into its rapture. Although it may not consciously register at the time, you learn that love is openness, acceptance, and joy.

To experience more Fulfilling Connections in everyday life, however, you usually need to make a conscious decision to learn. To continue with the falling-in-love example, you could make a choice to learn what allowed your love to triumph over your fears, what beliefs activated those fears and protections, and what you could do to disempower your fears. It is by knowing about the elements that create Fulfilling Connections that you become aware of what is missing when you are disconnected from your heart.

Underlying the openness necessary for Heart Learning is the assumption that, in any difficulty, there is something valuable to be learned, some opportunity to explore and develop Heart Feelings. This openness involves a sincere curiosity about yourself, your world, and the people with whom you come into contact.

Inscribed on the shrine of the Oracle of Delphi are the words "Know thyself." The original meaning of "to know," which comes from the

Hebrew word "yadar," is to have an intimate experience of something. To go beyond the surface of cognitive knowing and to deeply know yourself, you must plumb the infinite reaches of inner space.

This inevitably brings us face to face with the parts of ourselves that have been repressed to avoid criticism and rejection, both our own and from others. Until these parts are confronted, we need to protect ourselves from having those parts touched or exposed. When the goal of protection is paramount, we cannot allow ourselves to experience what we fear.

Self-protection, meaning disconnection from our Heart Feelings, is one of our earliest decisions. To learn more about our Heart Feelings and to more fully embrace them, it may be helpful to understand more about why we disconnected from them. This may require a trip back into childhood, to explore and possibly re-experience the pain of being a sensitive and passionate person.

If we were to have felt the pain every time parents, siblings, friends, relatives, and teachers disrespected us, which research suggests occurs many times each day, the pain would have been overwhelming. Instead, our minds created ways of seeing the world and blocking out the pain that allowed us to survive. Survive we did, but the scars now inhibit our ability to access our Heart Feelings.

One common way to protect ourselves from the vulnerability of our Heart Feelings is to push them deeply inside and become either unfeeling or to allow only those feelings and behaviors which we think will not leave us vulnerable. When hard feelings are present, we experience the dark side of ourselves. This too must be kept under wraps, repressed into the shadows. Denying both the "Darth Vadar" parts of us and our Heart Feelings leaves us without a real identity and without true personal power.

Embracing our disowned parts reduces their power, but confronting personal demons is scary. As a result, when it comes to learning about the parts of ourselves we fear, we all struggle with severe "learning disabilities."

However unpleasant, unless you are open to learning about your dark side, the feelings and behaviors it evokes will rarely be confronted or resolved, and opportunities for becoming your own hero and Fulfilling Connections are missed. Just as an archer can learn valuable lessons each time the bull's eye is missed, each time your heart closes, that experience can be used to learn about yourself.

When disconnected feelings and behaviors arise, will power alone is almost never enough to change them. For example, consider the times you decided not to eat a food you really love while keeping it in plain sight, or when you have vowed to never again get angry or feel jealous. There is another way.

After disconnected feelings and behavior have been expressed, opening to Heart Learning can give you a new perspective. This is the step most people miss. Typically, after failing at attempts to not feel or behave in a certain way, people attempt to whitewash the mess and then return to "business as usual," hoping that the feelings or behavior will not happen again. This may include sincere apologies and promises to not behave in that way again. But, without learning about and resolving the fears and beliefs that cause disconnected feelings and behaviors, the cycle is destined to be repeated.

Remembering that we created disconnected feelings and behavior as a protection to shield us from our suffering helps reform the tendency to judge ourselves. As adults, we are capable of handling feelings and situations that might have been devastating for us as children. However, even though we may no longer need our disconnected feelings and behaviors, they are hard-wired into our brains. They occur with such immediacy that they seem natural. They are not natural, and they can be rewired. But, because they happen so automatically and unconsciously, acknowledging them first is crucial for success.

Employing your experiences of disconnection to continually deepen your learning about yourself, others, and the world around you will lead to the many thorny questions that arise when you become an active participant in shaping your life—questions like:

- Who am I really, in my essence, beyond my roles and stories?
- What do I think I need?
- What is my habitual way of trying to get what I need?
- What unhappiness is created by my attempts to control?
- What would it mean to reduce my attempts to have control over events and people and to live with more faith?
- What is the meaning of life, and what is my place in it?

The answers to these and many other profound questions provide pieces for a puzzle that might be entitled "Fulfillment." It is a puzzle that you may never totally finish, but the more of it you complete, the more satisfaction you will achieve.

If we are to blossom, the repressed aspects of ourselves need our attention. With nurturing, wounds can heal, hidden abilities can emerge, and more Fulfilling Connections can result. Others can assist in creating an environment of safety, which allows us to bring our shadows into the light, and we can assist others to do the same; but no one can do the job for us. This is why we must learn to nurture ourselves.

The story that follows is about a young woman confronting her fears and learning to better nurture herself and become her own hero. It is the first of five "teaching stories." Other teaching stories appear in Chapters Four through Seven. Although the teaching stories are fiction, they are based upon actual case histories. Stories are used because they offer information in a way that is often more interesting, engaging, and easy to understand than information that is presented in a linear, more "intellectual" manner.

Each story is divided into three parts:

Differences, Disconnection, and Struggle—This section describes some of the commonly identifiable difficulties that are suffered when upsetting situations disconnect us from our hearts and send us into the darkness of our fears.

Heart Learning—In this part of the story each of the main characters uses different resources to connect with his or her heart. It is designed to illustrate some of the various paths that can be used in the pursuit of learning to overcome our fears.

Being Your Own Hero, Fulfilling Connections, and Possibilities— The final section portrays some of the transformational possibilities that can emerge as we step into the light of connecting by heart with others and ourselves.

TEACHING STORY #1

I Am a Dysfunctional Family

Differences, Disconnection, and Struggle

Awaiting her first opportunity to compete in a ballroom dance contest, Shawna grinned inwardly as she looked around the hall at the colorfully costumed women and smartly tuxedoed men. When the smile extended below her navel, a quick quiver caused her to simultaneously squirm, laugh out loud, and involuntarily strengthen her grip on her partner's hand.

Alan looked at her quizzically. "What's so funny?"

With cheeks flushed, eyes wide, and lips pressed into a coquettish smile, she looked like the cat who swallowed the canary as she coyly said, "Oh, I was just enjoying being here."

After a brief pause she continued more contemplatively, "I was also thinking about all the things that had to happen for me to be here, in this moment, with you." She paused for a moment and then brightened as she said, "Even though some of those things were pretty awful, look at me now! It's pretty amazing."

Smoothing her hair, Shawna lapsed back into silence. Feeling a little conceited, she thought to herself, "I wouldn't have looked so svelte and sexy in this dress thirty pounds ago." That thought had barely finished before her breath got caught in the thought, "Is it okay to feel proud?"

Her inner voice immediately reassured her, "Of course, whatever you feel is okay." Shawna sighed. It wasn't so long ago that her inner voice would have sounded like a critical parent punishing her for "bad thoughts," and anything egotistical was surely a no-no.

Her parents, Sam and Jill, deserved their reputation for modeling the principles of hard work and high morals. Sam's hardware store had furnished most of the supplies that fueled the town's enormous growth. After serving as a member of the school board for ten years, he was next elected to the city council, and eventually he became mayor.

Jill's inexhaustible energy made her the most visible woman in town. Volunteering for many fund-raising events, running Sam's election campaigns, organizing environmental clean-up efforts, and playing an active role in school events, she often seemed to be in two places at the same time. Folklore had it that she was a twin.

Even with overflowing plates of extracurricular activities, Sam and Jill always made sure they had enough time for parenting Shawna. They closely shepherded her through her childhood, while instilling in her a very well-defined code of conduct. Without an abiding connection to their compassion, however, the strict and vigilant imposition of their rules rarely considered Shawna's feelings. In addition, they, along with many other wellmeaning community members, were ever ready to give Shawna advice regarding how to live a better life and how to solve her own problems.

Shawna was the "perfect child," a sweet little girl who made her parents and her community proud. She always dressed appropriately, wearing her hair neatly pulled back into a ponytail, and the big smile that wrinkled her button nose was readily available. She also was an excellent student.

Then it happened. An event that, while it did not seem like such a big deal at the time, emblazoned in her the dire consequences that might result from making a mistake. Shawna was in the fourth grade when one evening she found herself torn between wanting to complete a report with her usual perfection and needing time to study for a test. As the evening wore on, she found herself becoming more and more tense.

At last, rather than master the material she was researching and write a report in her own words, she copied some material straight out of one of the reference books. She spent a fitful night. The next day she showed up with a few hairs uncharacteristically out of place. Shawna had no way of knowing that the book she plagiarized was one very familiar to her teacher. So, the first time she broke the rules, poor Shawna got caught.

After the school called with the news, Jill called Sam at the store and told him what had happened. He was mortified. His tightly controlled life had always gone his way before. Now, for the first time, he felt out of control and he became unglued. Obsessive thoughts raced through his head. "Why?" "What will people think?" "What should we do?" "Is this the beginning of yet worse behavior?" "What will become of my reputation?" His ruminations led to the firm resolve that he had better nip this in the bud before Shawna became one of those "out of control" teenagers.

He managed to finish the day, but by the time he got home he had whipped himself into a frenzy and his rage exploded onto Shawna. It terrified her. Fearing that he might hit her, she hid behind her mother. But that fear was nothing compared to the iciness she experienced over the next few days, as her father remained stern and distant, taking every available opportunity to let her know how disappointed he was in her.

Jill became depressed, and that just made things worse for Shawna. Shawna had experienced her mother's depression before, but it had been infrequent and had never lasted for more than a few hours. During those times Jill would become increasingly incapable of coping with life, and Shawna, feeling responsible, would take over. Shawna had discovered that sharing her latest accomplishments and her plans for the future comforted her mom and would usually bring back her mom's vivacious self.

This time, however, nothing she said could lift the curtain of Jill's darkness. It went on for so long that Shawna worried that it might never end. By the time the depression lifted, Shawna had become more convinced than ever that she alone was responsible for her mom's well-being. She fervently committed herself never to do anything that would upset her mom.

Shawna survived childhood and finished college with honors. She began her climb up the ladder of success on a high rung with a very good position at a large company. She kept her happy face turned toward the outer world, and even at the rare times when tears did fill her eyes, her mouth still turned up in the smile that wrinkled her nose.

To the outside world Shawna seemed happy and successful, but a gnawing discontent lurked internally. She was ever vigilant for signs of discomfort in others and felt guilty if her behavior seemed to cause another person any discomfort. She was adept at quickly changing any behavior that might make another unhappy, but she was not very good at identifying what it was that made her unhappy.

Being disconnected from self-compassion allowed her internal critic, the internalized hard, taskmaster parent, to quickly rise up and criticize her for not living up to her internalized standards and for hurting others. Her guilt was a constant reminder that she was both unlovable and inadequate. Unable to access the compassion that would allow her to accept her feelings and behavior, she was unable to nurture herself. This left her feeling a constant dullness, which was later identified as a mild depression.

Shawna spent the majority of her free time relentlessly searching for a magical cure for her restlessness. Her compulsive fight with her weight (which had begun in the fifth grade) sent her into many hours at the gym and into every new diet craze. Having learned to distrust her feelings and any knowledge that would have come from them, she was left with seeking others to tell her what was right. She plunged into one spiritual movement after another, always becoming the shining devotee on an ever-changing merry-go-round of charismatic gurus.

Shawna spent many years in therapy immersed in learning about the dysfunctional family in which she grew up. She voraciously read self-help books and sought out the help of a well-known psycho-therapist. All her efforts produced little relief for her depression.

Shawna's odyssey to learn more about love was a lonely journey. She was very shy, and she rarely reached out to people. Finally, in her late twenties, a person she barely knew at work asked her if she would like to go out one night. This colleague, Jessica, told her about a place she had been going to called the Center for Connection in Community (CCC). It was dedicated to helping people connect in more meaningful ways. Shawna, usually willing to try something new, agreed to go to an introductory evening.

Heart Learning

Shawna's experiences at CCC turned her life around. Before going to the introductory evening she had read the brochure describing the center. She was particularly taken by the following:

"Classes reflect the pursuit of intellectual inquiry within a framework of experiential learning. They are structured to foster safe, dynamic, and creative learning communities that encourage each individual's uniqueness. The relationship skills needed to embody this ideal are practiced within each class. To fulfill a commitment to the larger community, courses will afford opportunities for each person to address how they can be more responsible to, and better serve, society.

"Community events will illuminate the practices of a support community and are geared to deepen our understanding of our values. Events might include: a book club; movie and video clubs; discussion groups on topics such as parenting or politics; guest speakers and discussion; holiday rituals; game nights; dance lessons; dances; movement classes; and community dinners.

"All events are learning opportunities and will be evaluated by whether they fit the criteria of a support community, and by how in the future they can better serve the community. For example: Books and movies will be chosen that reflect the values of CCC; game nights might lead to discussions about what gets in the way of fun, e.g., our beliefs about competition, or our fears of letting go. Other community offerings might include: interpersonal learning groups for resolving conflicts and learning how to better live our values; and intergenerational involvement through mentoring and community events."

By the end of her first evening at CCC, Shawna knew she had finally found a home. In addition to finding a place that offered many things that were of interest to her, there seemed to be a philosophy that was more accepting of individual differences.

While perusing the bulletin board her eyes fixed on a flyer for a six-week class entitled "Relationship and Connection." When she read the line, "Learn about how to better nurture yourself and establish more intimate relationships with others," she knew this was for her.

On the first night, the teacher said, "In a minute I'm going to uncover a statement that's on this flip chart. It may not be absolutely true, but see if you can get beyond that concern and spend a few minutes writing what it means to you." He uncovered the following statement:

"Although you left your family of origin many years ago, you still carry it around in your head. Your internalized critical parent is responsible for your unhappiness."

Shawna felt a shiver of recognition go through her. The statement seemed to make unnessessary most of the time and effort she had put into thinking about what her parents had done to her. She was immediately struck by the realization that it was a transformational idea. She busily wrote down some initial thoughts that she intuitively knew would continually deepen.

During the rest of the class people shared their thoughts. By the end of the evening, Shawna had realized that concentrating on quieting her internal critic and doing a better job of being more loving toward herself would free her from rehashing the past, assigning blame, or trying to get anyone else to change. She left the class still spinning from the fertile information she had received.

On the way home she chuckled as she declared to herself, "I am a dysfunctional family." Although it would be a few more weeks before she felt comfortable enough to share this idea in class, with this realization she assumed the power to change.

Her teacher suggested some books that he thought would be helpful. With the combination of the books and the class, Shawna began unlearning old ideas and learning new ones. She found one of them, *The Dark Side of Light Chasers* by Debbie Ford, particularly helpful for revealing her shadow side and accepting more of herself.

She learned that nurturing herself meant being the compassionate parent to herself that she had always wanted her mother and father to be. She learned to access an inner wisdom that affirmed her thoughts and feelings and did not blame others for her unhappiness, thus taking responsibility for her own feelings. Any time she was able to this, she gave herself something of great value and felt totally peaceful.

To become more consistent in being more loving to herself, she realized that she would have to reprogram her beliefs about perfection. Believing that she was responsible for the feelings of others and for the choices they made usually left her feeling guilty and bad about herself. No matter what she accomplished, there was always the dangling carrot that if she just did better, she would get the love and approval she so desperately wanted. Now she had to learn to give that acceptance and self-love to herself, no matter how others reacted to what she did. With a guilt-inducing mother as her primary role model, this was a challenging proposition.

The punitive parent residing in her head—a generous blend of her mother and father—carried on the nonstop emotional abuse of criticism, advice, and threats. Furthermore, by heaping copious amounts of guilt and blame on herself when others were unhappy, Shawna herself reinforced the feelings she had of unworthiness and unloveability.

Shawna had always struggled with feelings of being unloved. Everyone in her life had told her how lucky she was to have such caring and involved parents. Her parents made a point of letting her know how much they sacrificed for her, how important she was to them, and how happy she made them. Shawna believed that her parents loved her and felt guilty when those nagging feelings of being unseen and unloved surfaced. She tried to suppress those feelings and had never shared them with anyone.

Nurturing herself meant seeing her parents from a new perspective. She learned that underneath her parents' controlling behavior, they were both very frightened. Her father's fluctuations between emotional distance and anger masked his terror of being controlled. Her mother's depression, well-meaning advice, and sharing of her feelings masked her own feelings of powerlessness and fear that, if Shawna developed her own power, Shawna would also end up alone and lonely. Although not conscious, her parents' efforts at protection were attempts to get Shawna not to do the things that might bring about their worst fears.

Jill, unwilling to feel her pain, never took responsibility for her own feelings nor wanted to search for the real causes of her unhappiness—her disconnecting beliefs. Instead, she always tried getting others to make her feel better. This practice encouraged Shawna in her belief that she was responsible for her mother's depression. Cut off from her self-compassion, Jill rarely felt compassion for Shawna.

In the new light of these ideas Shawna had this realization: "No wonder I've felt unseen, ungrateful, bad about myself, and unloved."

Her teacher had put up a list of ideas from which these thoughts had germinated. She put the list on her refrigerator:

1. Compassion communicates that you are always doing the best you can.
2. If a person giving advice doesn't know the very important reasons you have for doing what you are doing, or is not open to learning about them, compassion is not present.
3. Acceptance or an intent to learn communicates faith that although you are presently stuck, you will find the way through your difficulties.
4. Knowing that others have faith in you leaves you feeling loved. Regularly telling others what to do communicates the opposite.

A major shift in Shawna's behavior toward her mother occurred when she realized that self-compassion was what she needed to take better care of herself. Whereas in the past the only way she believed she could feel better was to get her mother to change, now she had another way. She began letting go of trying to get her mother to see things differently and change.

On the last night of class, the instructor asked each person to answer, "How is what you are learning affecting your feelings about yourself?" Shawna wrote the following: "I am feeling more in control of my life than I ever have, and it feels great."

Being Your Own Hero, Fulfilling Connections, and Possibilities

Not long after the class ended Shawna had an opportunity to put some of her new learning into practice. She was feeling frazzled from an interaction with her boss when her mother called. Jill asked, "How are you?" and Shawna told her what had just happened.

Jill's immediate response was, "Well, you know, darling, he probably is feeling a little threatened by you. You know how pushy you get at times. Why don't you just back off and try being softer with him?"

Shawna immediately felt her entire body lock in tension. She knew that in the past she would have reacted to her mother by either agreeing or getting angry, and with either one she would have been a victim. Instead, this time after a deep breath she saw the scared little girl behind her mother's facade. That compassion, and the security of knowing that she had the right to stand up for herself and thus maintain her integrity, combined to produce a simple and gentle, "Mom, I'm really not needing your advice. What I'd really love is for you just to hear me. Can you do that?"

Jill tried, "Of course I can, darling, but you know you can catch a lot more bees with honey than with vinegar," and unfortunately she failed. To give Shawna what she was wanting, Jill would have had to feel compassion. Since that might have opened her to feelings, such as her unhappiness, that she was not ready to confront, she protected herself behind pat homilies and timeworn advice.

Shawna knew that, to nurture to herself, she needed to get out of range of her mother's verbal assaults. She had given her mother a chance to open her heart. Had that happened, they would have had a wonderful conversation and would have likely felt very close to each other. Instead, only Shawna's heart stayed open. In nurturing herself, however, she felt terrific.

As Shawna became more connected to her Heart Feelings, many changes began to occur. Her eating habits changed, and slowly, without even trying to diet, she began to lose weight. Her loving energy radiated. She touched people in new ways and she noticed people reacting differently to her. She found herself being interested in things to which she had been indifferent in the past.

One day Jessica suggested they watch the film *Strictly Ballroom*. "It's one of my all-time favorites; you'll love it," Jessica said.

"What's it about?" asked Shawna.

"Well, it's actually an Australian farce about ballroom dancing."

Shawna had never thought much about dancing; in fact, the thought of it was rather scary. She had never considered herself particularly graceful or feminine, both attributes that she associated closely with dancing.

Watching the film boggled her mind. Something about the sound and rhythms of the Latin music touched her in a way that she had never experienced before. She couldn't stop smiling, and her body seemed to have a mind of its own as she danced in her seat. As the credits rolled, she and Jessica got up and spontaneously moved together to the music.

"That was so much fun. I want to do it some more!" Shawna exclaimed with more genuine joy than she had ever felt.

"Well," Jessica coyly said, "I've been taking a class at CCC called "The Dance Connection." I wanted to see if you were interested in coming, but I thought you might reject the idea if I asked you directly. I got hooked on ballroom dancing after I saw this movie, so I decided to try it out on you. I hope you're not upset with me for not being totally up-front with you."

"You know, you're probably right. If you had just said, 'Come to the class,' I probably would have made some excuse. But now I'm hot to trot. When does the next class start?"

"Every six weeks we start a new set of two dances. Right now we're learning salsa and nightclub two-step. Three weeks from Wednesday we begin learning tango and swing. If you want to have dinner after work, we could drive over together."

"It's a deal."

The next day Shawna bought some Latin music CDs and, before ever attending her first class, she found herself hooked on Latin music. She had it constantly playing on her stereo and, rather than walking from room to room, she danced her way across her apartment. The music connected to an unexplored, and previously unknown, part of her. It brought her feelings closer to the surface and allowed her to feel more sensual, and to laugh and cry more easily.

Getting out of her head and into her heart felt wonderful, indulgent, romantic, and naughty. She thought, "I don't know if this is what it means to be out of control, or if this is what my mother was frightened of, but I love it."

She couldn't get enough dance talk with Jessica. One evening they got together for dinner and to watch the film *Tango*. They were mesmerized.

"That was the most stunningly gorgeous film I have ever seen!" Jessica exclaimed.

"Yeah, the dancing was amazing, but the lighting and the costumes were incredible," Shawna added. "I can't wait for next Wednesday."

Her first night in class exceeded her expectations. Jeff, the teacher, was affable, encouraging, and very accepting. He began by saying, "For me, dancing is very basic and simple. It is letting a rhythm move your body. Partnership dancing is doing that with someone else. Connection happens when your heart is involved in this process. That's what this class will be all about."

Shawna's mind immediately recalled one of her favorite scenes from *Strictly Ballroom* when the grandmother asks the hotshot dancer, "Where do you feel the rhythm?" He replied by moving his feet. She stopped him, cupped her hands over his stomach and heart, and began to alternately beat out a cadence on his chest as she said, "Here, and here." After a few beats she said, "Listen to the rhythm. Don't be scared."

Shawna smiled, feeling as if she was in heaven, as if she had "come home."

All she had been hungering for was epitomized in the dancing. Dancing and music became vehicles for opening her heart and connecting to her compassion and joy. Those feelings nourished her. Whereas in the past she could nurture others, she had never known how to nurture herself, or how to allow herself to be nurtured by others. Now, each time she allowed herself to be touched physically and emotionally, it was fulfilling.

The more Shawna connected to her heart, the more the alienated parts of her developed and the more brightly she glowed. It was a transformation that changed her entire physical appearance. Just as her physical features became more striking as she lost the fat that had hidden them, unwrapping her internal beauty affected how everyone saw her.

Upon completing the beginning level, Jeff suggested to his new shining star that she join his advanced class. The first time she entered the studio many of the advanced students were already warming up. Her gaze stopped and her eyes fixed on a gorgeous hunk of a man doing ballet movements at the practice bar. He noticed her through the mirror, turned and glided over to greet this newest student. By the end of the class he had asked if she wanted to get a cup of coffee.

At the coffee shop, Alan said, "Have you seen *Shall We Dance?*"

She replied, "No, what's it about?"

"It's a Japanese film about a man who discovers new aspects about himself when he takes up ballroom dancing within a culture that distances itself from it. If you're interested in seeing it, I happen to own a copy of it."

"Sure, I'm interested. Sounds like the story of my life. When can we see it?"

"How about right now?"

She hesitated only a second. "Sure, why not?" It was 11:00 p.m., and Shawna had never acted so spontaneously in her life. But this moment encapsulated everything for which she had been working. She would savor it as long as she could.

Shawna and Alan became more than dance partners. The more she got to know him, the more she realized that the magnetic attraction that first night was the energy of this very special man. She discovered that he too had worked hard at overcoming the heart disconnection from which he had suffered.

She often found herself thinking, "Does everyone think he's as gorgeous as I do? Well, I guess it really doesn't matter. I just hope I always see him the same way."

Their love was like a fairytale; their life was not—at least not any more than any life is. It was a real relationship with differences and hiccups. The chance for keeping their love alive was anchored by their appreciation for what it had taken to get to the place where they were ready to love another person, and their commitment to maintaining an open heart connection with themselves and each other.

Nurturing Heart Feelings

Nurturing Heart Feelings is challenging because it requires encouraging the expression of *all* feelings, and the most terrifying freedom of all is the freedom to feel. Feelings can threaten the roles and rules prescribed by a culture. We fear that we might not be able to "attend to business" if we allow our feelings to be expressed. For example, men might be too sensitive. Women might be too sexual. We might realize how badly we feel when we are in situations that are emotionally and physically abusive or nonsupportive, and then we would have to confront those realities. We might not stay under the control of others and others might not stay under our control.

To stay within our boundaries, we believe that our feelings must be controlled. With that perspective, it is understandable why intellectual development is encouraged in our culture while expressing feelings is so

31

often discouraged. The fear of not being under the mind's control is one reason that the development of the mind is given much greater importance than the development of nonintellectual capacities.

Our culture encourages us to repress certain feelings. But feelings remind us of the uniqueness of being human. Like fluctuations on a life-support monitor, they reflect the highs and lows of life as they animate us both in ecstasy and pain. Contrast this to the flat line signifying the end of life that would appear on the monitor when feelings are completely repressed. This accurately describes those victims of acculturation who died a long time ago and are just waiting for the actual event to take place.

Becoming accepting of both Heart Feelings and disconnected feelings is how we nurture ourselves. This is typically more difficult with disconnected feelings, such as anger, jealousy, hatred, and greed. Learning what has alienated us from our compassion is the way toward reconnecting with our hearts. For Shawna it meant quieting her internal critic. Learning how to honor our feelings rather than critically judging ourselves for having them is a major part of Heart Learning. The weight of our beliefs about the rights and wrongs of feelings makes this an exceptionally challenging task.

Learning About Nurturing Heart Feelings

The environment that nurtures Heart Learning allows us to contemplate and decide what we want to learn and when we want to learn it. We already possess the ability to gather the information required to deal with troubling feelings and situations. Many times we even have the information, although it may be buried in our unconscious. Unconscious material may take some time to come to the surface, but when we are ready for it, it will become apparent.

People who tell us what we should do and how we should act and behave frustrate our ability to learn and help perpetuate our lack of self-esteem. People who help us uncover what we know nurture us by helping us trust our ability to learn and thus feel better about ourselves. Shawna found this kind of support in her relationships and her classes at CCC.

The experience of a spacious, safe, learning environment is rare. More often, our internal critic, or perhaps other people, pressure us to come up with answers, solutions, or changes in our behavior. Being pounced on with answers or theories usually inhibits coming up with conclusions that include Heart Feelings. Being told what to do robs us of the opportunity to figure things out for ourselves and communicates a lack of faith in our ability to solve our problems. Being pressured to see things we are not ready to see produces the dissonance that disconnects us from our Heart Feelings and Heart Learning.

Many well-meaning people often indulge in dispensing simplistic ideas. Ministers, gurus, teachers, psychologists, parents, grandparents, in-laws, friends often drown us in pat answers and common aphorisms, such as: An abusive woman should just not take it anymore and/or leave her husband. A financially dependent person on welfare should just get a job. An over-weight person should just go on a diet. Parents with delinquent children should just "get tough."

Upon seeing another person in a difficult situation, many of us can clearly see ways to get out of the unhappiness and freely express our ideas about how to act, think, and feel. Of course, it is not so simple to the one in difficulty. Simplistic solutions to complex problems, however, will most likely result in failure for the person having the difficulty and thus further erode his or her already fragile self-esteem. Advice does not usually help people feel better about themselves, and it is certainly not helpful in facilitating Heart Learning and connection to one's Heart Feelings.

You can begin building your learning sanctuary by reducing the propensity to cast yourself and others as being "wrong." The internal critic was the powerful force that Shawna confronted when she realized that she herself was a dysfunctional family.

How do you react toward yourself when you: make a mistake; forget something; do something that goes against what you believe to be "right"; waste time; or lose your temper? Does your internal critic run amok, using these instances as the perfect opportunity to convince you of how inadequate you are? Do you call yourself a jerk or stupid? If you are not free to feel, think or behave without fearing critical judgments, your internal environment is not safe.

Acceptance is the key to stimulating Heart Learning. Honoring your own and others' thoughts, feelings, and behavior comes from believing that there are always very important reasons for behavior. "Important reasons" are not excuses for behavior. Rather, they allow you to learn more about your own or another's actions so that you can deepen your understanding and gain the acceptance that moves you toward Fulfilling Connections and being your own hero.

The important reasons for behavior may not always be apparent to an observer, or even consciously known to the person exhibiting the behavior. But powerful fears and beliefs drive behavior that may seem inappropriate or hurtful. For example, were Jill, Shawna's mother, to confront that part of herself that was cold and selfish, her learning might have resulted in the following:

"I realize that I have often been critical or harsh with Shawna out of my own fears. Sometimes it's fear for her well-being, but it's also my own fear of losing control. Maybe I'm afraid that she would have to face the kind of hardships I went through as a young woman, and I want to prevent that. I justify my need for control by telling myself it's my responsibility as a parent to make sure my daughter follows a certain path. It makes me sad to think that my own fears result in a less loving relationship with my daughter."

An important part of encouraging Heart Learning is realizing and accepting that our motives are not always pure. Often our behavior has multiple, and sometimes conflicting, motives. For example, as a parent we may want to believe that our child's welfare is always at the core of our parenting decisions, but sometimes our actions have more to do with our own needs or fears than theirs. Only by making it acceptable for there to be multiple motives can you then admit to having a shadow side, and thus to prevent that shadow from co-opting your best efforts.

Sometimes merely acknowledging a new concept, like multiple motives, is enough to shift your behavior. However, if deeply ingrained judgments are in place, change may not be easy. Accepting that you may have "shadowy" motives often requires taking a close look at the beliefs perpetuating your fears. Discovering those beliefs and testing them out is the process illuminated in the next chapter.

Acknowledging the less flattering sides of you opens the door to self-acceptance. What difference would it make if, free of judgment, you could accept that in every loving act there was a part of you that was unloving, or that in every feeling of joy for a friend's good fortune there was a little bit of jealousy? What difference would it make if you could accept yourself as sometimes being controlling, judgmental, lazy, selfish, arrogant, forgetful, and uncaring?

By declaring your own demons and adding them to this unflattering list, you take another step in the ongoing process of creating a learning sanctuary. The kinder you can be to yourself, the more you will be able to confront those aspects of yourself that are creating disconnection and the sooner you will enjoy more Fulfilling Connections to yourself and others.

I remember the first time someone called me selfish. I became immediately defensive, and I began to recite everything I had done for that person. I called her ungrateful, along with a host of other more insulting, unflattering names. We had a major argument. I left the room filled with anger.

It was a long time before I could accept the part of me that feared the truth of my friend's accusation. I had to come to terms with realizing that even though I really loved being of service, giving, and making others happy, there were times when my self-interests were the primary motivation.

One valuable piece of information that really helped me came from a lecture I heard by Ram Dass. For many years he has been one of my most valued spiritual teachers, and his ideas have been a great help and comfort to me. In front of an auditorium full of people he said, "Sometimes my perversions come up and I look at them and say, 'There are my perversions again!'" To hear this man whom I saw as highly evolved and loving say that he had perversions began the process of making it okay for me to have my own dark places. I could now more easily admit to being selfish at times, and yet I still could acknowledge that I was a loving person.

In learning how to better create Heart Learning, you will find self-criticism giving way to understanding. Knowing the important reasons you have for acting and feeling as you do, you will come to feel compassion. Compassion creates the internal sanctuary that allows your heart to open and to accept yourself. The more accepting you are of yourself, the more accepting you will be of others. Compassionate acceptance of others likewise creates a safe place and opens the door for them to explore and accept themselves. With compassionate acceptance in place, the path toward being your own hero is cleared for takeoff.

Chapter Three

Living in the Mystery

Accepting uncertainty as our philosophy might allow us to honor each other's stories more, delighting in all the bizarre and wondrous interpretations of the mystery. We might also show more tolerance for those who appear to be fools, and for those who speak truths we don't wish to hear.

—Wes "Scoop" Nisker, *Crazy Wisdom*

The juice of Fulfilling Connections comes from the mystery of life working its magic. Without fear encasing our hearts we freely engage in the fullness of the moment. Captivated in the wonder of a fascinating adventure, we enjoy its surprises and challenges rather than attempting to protect ourselves from potential difficulties. We feel alive instead of bored, passionate instead of dead, serene instead of anxious. We are animated instead of blasé and active instead of passive.

When our abilities are empowered by Heart Feelings we are open to new possibilities. The policeman in Chapter One had a new awareness about his mission. When Shawna, in Chapter Two, nurtured herself with music and dance, she connected to unexplored parts of herself that allowed her to feel more sensual and to laugh and cry more easily. You will notice the phenomenon of awe-inspiring experiences that accompany living in the mystery happening to each of the main characters in the stories throughout this book. In real life, these experiences are sometimes labeled magic or miracles—but they routinely happen when a heart is open.

The receptivity of an open heart can be symbolized by the image of outstretched arms with the palms turned toward the heavens. In this image, fear is not predominant and the innocence and openness of living in the mystery is accompanied by softness, acceptance, and curiosity. It is a safe space for all thoughts, feelings, and actions. Differences are welcomed and honored. Questions and problems are important, but rather than being treated as burdens, they are embraced as opportunities. In the examples of the policeman with the lawbreaker, and of Shawna with her depressed mother, each acted from an open heart even though what presented itself could have been an occasion of challenge or fear.

As my personal story continues to unfold it will detail more of my journey toward living more connected to my Heart Feelings and becoming more of my own hero. The following part describes some of the dividends of living in the mystery. Later in this chapter I will share more of my own process of confronting and resolving some of my fears.

I'll never forget that June morning as I pulled out of my driveway at 4:30 a.m. and waved good-bye to my house, to the woman I had been married to for a quarter century, and to a long and successful career. The mixture of stark terror and hopeful excitement was like nothing I had ever felt before. Unlike many of the confident movie heroes of my childhood, who conquered the West and rode off into the sunset, I was unsurely driving into the sunrise. It was like I was in an "Eastern," and I felt more like Wrong Way Corrigan than John Wayne.

On the highway in Southern Utah, for the first time in my life, I drove off the main road and literally took the road less traveled. Alone, meandering through Zion National Park and Bryce Canyon, I was awestruck by a power and magnificence I had never before experienced.

Troubling questions, pain, doubt, and joy merged with the grandeur of God's sculptures, and a floodgate opened, releasing torrents of tears, both of gratitude and fear. The terror of leaving all the people on whom I had come to depend for emotional support, and the sadness of ending a relationship with the only woman with whom I had ever been in love, took a back seat to the exhilaration of launching the greatest adventure of my life.

The decision to separate from Margie had been terrifying, but one I was ready to make. The past year had been extremely difficult, but I had come through it pretty well. The initial devastation I had felt when Margie announced that she wanted to separate was beginning to subside. In addition to my weekly therapy appointments, I had gained additional insights from attending Marianne Williamson's Sunday night lectures on *A Course in Miracles* and much-needed support from a men's group I had joined.

It felt especially good to turn to men for support. During my entire lifetime I had only known women as the nurturers. I had always felt much more comfortable allowing women to see my softer side. Now I was beginning to trust men, and, in the process, learning to trust and nurture myself.

I began my new life in the mountains of Colorado. Living in a small town connected me to the earth and to people in an entirely new way. My rear balcony was directly above the Roaring Fork River (named for the roar that occurred every spring as it swelled from the snowmelt). My front balcony looked directly out toward Aspen Mountain.

In Los Angeles I had felt anonymous, and maintaining friendships was a chore. People typically made dates to see each other two or three weeks in advance, met for lunch or dinner, and then didn't see each other for months. Here, making friends was easy and keeping up those friendships occurred naturally. I either walked or rode my bike to downtown and was always bumping into people I knew at restaurants, in movie theaters, or on the ski slopes. It was like being on a college campus. I discovered a gregarious part of myself that I never knew existed, and I loved it.

For the first time since high school, I established a "best friendship" with a male. Lee was the first heterosexual man I had ever known who had developed and balanced the many sides of himself. He was a successful businessman and a creative artist, a skilled athlete and very sensitive, and an intellectual who was not afraid of looking foolish.

The friendship encouraged me to uncover my heart and discover many new parts of myself. One of these was my ability to play and have fun. I had always been a very serious, "nose to the grindstone," responsible and productive kind of guy. Lee, on the other hand, was very comfortable playing naturally and noncompetitively like a child.

One day while walking along a snow-covered trail, Lee fell into the snow and spontaneously began laughing, screaming, and rolling down the hill. When he got to the bottom he yelled, "What are you waiting for?"

I gulped and launched myself into the snow bank, tumbling down toward him as he waited, snowball in hand. We ran and threw snowballs until we collapsed giggling in a heap.

"You're pretty good at this!" Lee chided.

I grinned. "That was really fun. I haven't done anything like that since I was a kid."

"Well, when you let go," Lee took a breath and, calling up his best Forest Gump imitation, continued, "it's like a box of chocolates. You never know what you're going to get. Sometimes it's magic. There certainly are no guarantees, but it's always an adventure."

As I looked in awe at this "Yoda" in front of me, I was filled with gratitude for the perfection of this moment.

Our "magical mystery tour" extended into everything we did. At parties I allowed myself to dance freely, giving my body permission to gyrate in ways that felt connected to my internal rhythm. Biking, hiking, listening to concerts, watching sunsets and sunrises, looking at the stars, having philosophical discussions, and reading poetry—all flowed easily and joyfully.

I also discovered a serenity and openness I had never before known. I started writing poetry for the first time in my life and was constantly surprised by the images that flowed from me. Tears streamed like never before. I was deeply moved by nature, films, or when talking about my family. And I laughed a lot. One night I met a woman at a party, and in the course of the evening she said, "I never heard a man giggle before." I thought for a moment and then replied, "I never giggled before I moved here, but I love it."

One day while on a chair lift, Lee and I began one of our now routine philosophical discussions. Still deeply engrossed when we reached the top of the run, Lee gestured toward the out-of-bounds fence and suggested we talk for a while. We skied to a deserted spot, took off our skis, and sat on a snow-covered rock.

I continued where we had left off. "You know, the more I allow things to unfold and don't try to plan everything or have control over things, the more peaceful I feel. Do you know what I mean?"

"Well, I'm not sure because I haven't known you for that long. But do you mean you're feeling more open and less defensive?" Lee asked.

"Yeah. It seems like the more open I am, the more secure I feel. I think that the more I know that I'm not dependent on anything or anyone outside myself for my sense of well-being, the more I'm gaining a faith that I've never known before. I feel a connection to God in a new way. I'm not even sure what I mean when I use the term 'God', but as I come to appreciate the supreme intelligence that created all this, I find myself comfortable thinking about God for the first time in my life."

Seeing that I was deep in thought, Lee didn't respond, and we sat quietly for a few minutes. Finally, I continued, "You know, I feel a humility in knowing that there are many things beyond my ability to know. Perhaps a Supreme Being knows these answers, and perhaps not. It doesn't matter. I think that the most important thing is just being the most loving person I can be. If there's a heaven, being open and loving should be enough to get me there. And if this lifetime is all there is, then so be it. I'm feeling so good that I wouldn't change a thing."

"Wow," Lee responded. "For a Tuesday morning at the top of the mountain, that's pretty deep, dude."

We looked at each other and started laughing. I really appreciated the way Lee allowed his learning to stay focused while he brought lightness into even our weightiest discussions. The thought of two men deeply sharing their thoughts and feelings caused my head to nod slightly in disbelief.

We buckled our boots, stepped into our skis, and began poling back toward the top of the ski run. I said, "Another thing I just thought of: Margie used to accuse me of not being on a spiritual path because I didn't believe in things like past lives, spirit guides, and angels. I'm beginning to think that maybe it's just that our paths are different and that neither of us is right or wrong."

"Your path is definitely unique," Lee responded, "and that can probably be said of most, if not all, of us. I don't know what spirituality is, but it seems to me that playing God by pretending to know things that only God could know definitely doesn't seem spiritual."

As I thought about this, I realized that staying open and loving with others and truly respecting their beliefs as just as true as mine would make a great difference in my life. I thought, "Maybe living with that kind of humility is my spiritual path."

I wanted to share this with Lee, but musing had slowed me considerably. Lee, an expert skier, was already at the Black Diamond sign that signaled an advanced run. He yelled over his shoulder, "I'm going to ski the bumps. I'll meet you at the bottom." With a "Yahoo!" he took off and disappeared from sight.

I smiled as I tucked my last thought away in my "to be shared later file." As confirmation that my path was different, I took off down a leisurely slope, silently slithering in six inches of new powder while fully reveling in the glow of the glistening snow-covered branches.

Beliefs—The Key to Increasing the Moments of Being Your Own Hero

Expanding our time in the mystery brings us face to face with our most formidable obstacle—our own minds. The human brain, which has the incredible ability to think abstractly and create wondrous ideas, also has the ability to create the beliefs and fears that disconnect us from our Heart Feelings.

As stated earlier, when we believe we are unable to handle the loss of something, our hearts close and attempts to control things and people persist. The fears that disconnect us from Heart Feelings and take us out of the mystery are created by beliefs. Examples of disconnecting beliefs are: "I am flawed, unlovable, and incapable of creating my own sense of well-being if [fill in the blank] occurs;" or "I am responsible for another person's feelings."

Disconnecting beliefs create the judgments that make actions, thoughts, and feelings wrong and create the limiting patterns that imprison us. When they hold sway, celebrating the good fortune of others gives way to jealousy; seeing the magnificence of our mates gives way to withdrawing in silence; looking at our children and bathing in their glory gives way to enforcing a lesson.

As the hold of disconnecting beliefs is loosened, we connect more often to our Heart Feelings and gain the strength to stand proudly as we really are. The following two sections look at two aspects of beliefs that disconnect us from our Heart Feelings: first, what we believe, and second, being rigidly attached to the sanctity of our beliefs.

Beliefs that allow living in the mystery permit actions, thoughts, and feelings to be regarded with reverence. They are beliefs like: "I am a worthwhile, lovable person and capable of creating my own sense of well-being if [fill in the blank] occurs;" and "I am not responsible or at fault for how another person reacts to something I have done, but I am responsible for how I respond to their reaction." Beliefs that nurture the expression of Heart Feelings will be referred to here as Connecting Beliefs, and the opposite beliefs are, of course, Disconnecting Beliefs.

Disconnecting Beliefs are established when feelings are not nurtured. For example, when our natural ability to feel compassion is ridiculed, we may create the belief that it is wrong to be sensitive and caring. Or, should our compassion lead us to be taken advantage of because we have not nurtured ourselves, we may create the belief that we cannot allow ourselves to be compassionate.

Beliefs that translate into "right" ways to think and act occur when we disconnect from compassion. This often occurs around beliefs regarding behavior. This might be a critical judgment about how someone looked or acted, a spoken word that was believed to be inappropriate, clothes worn that were believed to be hideous, or how someone may have been addressed in a way that was believed to be rude.

Defining certain behaviors as "right" or "normal" makes all other behavior wrong and abnormal and inevitably leads to attempting to impose one's own beliefs on others. Being "right" does not convey the caring, respect, warmth, acceptance, and embracing of compassion, and typically results in the eruption of "holy wars" across continents and dinner tables; or it may result, just as destructively, in acquiescent capitulation.

Disconnecting Beliefs are continually reinforced throughout our lives. They often become the "common sense" ideas about the right way to behave, think, and feel that are so deeply embedded that their seeming truth is not questioned. This makes them highly resistant to change.

In *Hamlet*, Shakespeare advises us that ". . . for there is nothing either good or bad but thinking makes it so." So it is only our immovable belief systems that seem to make things right or wrong. Words, manners, and ideas, just like the stereotypical traits that define masculine and feminine, are arbitrary. We make them up ourselves or adopt them from other people and they change with time and interpretation.

Take a moment and consider what it would mean if you were to believe, as Chuang Tzu suggests in *The Complete Works of Chuang Tzu*, that "Right is not right; so is not so. If right were really right, it would differ so clearly from not right that there would be no need for argument. If so were really so, it would differ so clearly from not so that there would be no need for argument. Forget the years; forget distinctions. Leap into the boundless and make it your home!"

With true compassion, behavior cannot be put into categories of right and wrong. In Chapter One it was noted that compassion is a central idea in all prevailing spiritual disciplines and that Jesus saw compassion as the central quality of God. If that is so, a compassionate God could not be disapproving but would rather lovingly embrace everyone and all their diversity. There could not be any sins or sinners. There could only be people struggling with the consequences of becoming disconnected from their compassion. The only hell that could occur would be when we lose compassion. With compassion, there would be sorrow for those who have lost their way, but there would never be criticism or anger.

To increase Fulfilling Connections in your life, it is important to look at whether beliefs connect or disconnect you from your Heart Feelings. Does a belief create the freedom and open heart of love, or does it create the imprisoning, closed protectiveness of fear? An exercise for evaluating beliefs is in the appendix as part of The Fulfilling Connections Process.

Part of a commitment to living in the mystery more of the time means learning what it means to become more comfortable swimming in a sea of questions rather than standing rigidly on islands of concrete beliefs, especially about things that are beyond our capacity to know with absolute certainty. The myriad of things beyond our capacity to know with absolute certainty comprises the mystery of life. That mystery is illuminated by innumerable questions: What is the essence of human beings and of life itself? What behavior is right and what is wrong? What things lie beyond our consciousness and our ability to perceive with our senses? What causes illness and what heals us? What happens after death? And, of course, the ultimate mystery from which the answers to many unknowable questions are drawn: Who is God?

Since the loss of Heart Feelings is directly affected by our beliefs and how we hold them, the quest for more Fulfilling Connections depends on how we handle the unknowable. Once answers to unanswerable questions are believed to be "the truth," it is a short step to attempting to convince others to believe it.

But even if we do not attempt to impose our beliefs on others, holding them as universal truths rather than personal truths immediately disconnects us from the compassionate acceptance and respect of our Heart Feelings. Beliefs like "There are no coincidences," "Whatever happens to you is part of God's plan," or "After you die you go into the light and then . . .[fill in the blank here]" are opinions that can be comforting and can have a positive effect in one's life. However, when these beliefs are held as facts, then having compassionate empathy, acceptance, and respect for those who do not share those opinions is impossible, and distance and alienation must follow.

I heard a popular motivational speaker say in one of his seminars, "Whenever my wife and I are having difficulties with our children, we tell them that everyone chooses the family they are born into." This concept is not expressed as an idea but as a fact. But how can he be sure? And, if he is speaking "the truth," what does it say about those who do not believe they chose their family? Or, when those in his audience accept the idea that we choose our birth family as the truth, what happens when it is expressed to others who do not believe it? This seemingly innocuous example illustrates some of the potential difficulties caused by teaching beliefs as if they are facts.

Even though many of our beliefs cannot be determined to be "true" in any absolute way, they are often held as facts rather than beliefs. Once we believe something to be a fact, we become invested in the rightness of it and harden in the face of alternative ideas. The compassion of Heart Learning is then lost and those who do not agree with our "truths" are wrong, or we make ourselves wrong when we do not live up to our beliefs.

We may believe that we are accepting of differences, but once we have discovered "a truth," it is uncompromising and, therefore, anything else is not the truth. Our way is the "right" way, and those who do not see things that particular way are misinformed and, therefore, wrong. If there is only one truth, how could it be any other way?

In *One*, Richard Bach devotes a fascinating chapter to the consequences of holding beliefs as the truth. In it, Jean-Paul Le Clerc gives Richard pages that contain truths called the "Light of Love." Richard is awed, and in his desire to serve humanity wants to give these words of wisdom to the world.

Le Clerc guides him through a chain of events that describe what will happen. They begin by naming the truths "The Pages." The following is a portion of their dialogue:

Le Clerc asks Richard, "And will you safeguard The Pages? Or will you allow others to edit them, to change what they don't understand, to strike out what they please, whatever is not to their liking?"

Richard replies, "No! No changes. They were delivered from the light! No changes!"

"Are you sure? Not a line here and there, for good reason? Most people won't understand? This might offend? The message isn't clear?"

"No changes!"

After a few more exchanges that explore how the words will be protected, Le Clerc says, "And here begins the Pageite priesthood. Those who give their lives to protect an order of thinking become the priests of that order. Yet any new order, any new way, is change. And change is the end of the world as it is."

A few more exchanges describe those people who will be threatened by the truth contained in The Pages and who will attempt to silence Richard. Le Clerc asks him, "And when you're followed, and caught, and cornered?"

"If I have to fight, I'll fight. There are principles more important than life. Some ideas are worth dying for."

The old man sighed, "And so began the Pageite Wars."

When living in the mystery, we gratefully and humbly accept any information we are given without the necessity of naming it and creating a story about where it came from. Dreams, voices, and visions are gifts and wonders to be used in whatever way serves us to become more loving. We can have fun with the information and play with the myriad possibilities of where they may have come from, but as soon as we become attached to a particular interpretation we leave the mystery and become subject to the arguments, distance, and the lack of Fulfilling Connections that result from rigidly held beliefs.

Being freed from trying to determine a single truth allows appreciation for the gift of divergent views that we have been given. Just imagine a world where religions hold their doctrines as choices rather than as God-given or divinely inspired absolute truths.

Holding beliefs as choices, not facts, acknowledges that they are a subjective reality, which you have chosen. "I choose to believe there are spirit guides" is very different than "There are spirit guides." When lightly held, beliefs are not attached to sanctity, but acknowledged as *your* truth, not *the* truth.

The Indian spiritual guru Jiddu Krishnamurti said, "The highest form of human intelligence is the ability to observe without evaluating." When living in the mystery, although solutions are not the focus, meaningful answers come naturally and effortlessly. These answers are not taken as "gospel" but are seen as transitory. They are merely door openers for other questions.

Inhabiting the unknown and constructing ideas to explain the unexplainable is understandable. In the face of fears that lie in the unknown, using our intellect in an attempt to feel safe makes perfect sense. But there is a price to pay—our attempts to have control over life block the flow that connects us to our Heart Feelings, others, and to Spirit.

Control

To more completely understand living in the mystery, the issue of control must be given serious consideration. For most of us, the thought of being out of control is so terrifying that we try to avoid it at all costs. The powerful desire to protect ourselves from our fears is revealed by the vast number of ways we try to gain control over future events.

Assigning meaning to life's imponderables is a common and seemingly natural attempt at control. Living with the unknown was perhaps so terrifying to our ancestors that they gave it meaning and a reality. They developed elaborate constructions about God, death, and about how the universe works. Now we are left to choose from their myriad interpretations about the future, some of which give us comfort and some of which give us fear. Either way, we mistakenly hope that knowing "the truth" will arm us for the future.

Another example of a desire for control is the penchant to seek and follow the advice of those who claim to predict the future. First, we create the illusion that we can simplify life, make it understandable, and thus have control over it. Then, in our insatiable pursuit of answers about things that are unknowable, we seek many kinds of experts:

- Religious leaders to tell us who and what God is and what happens after death
- Practitioners of the healing arts to tell us why people get sick
- Psychotherapists to tell us how to live our lives
- Gurus, psychics, channels, astrologers, and tarot card readers to tell us what will happen and how we will feel or act in the future
- Authorities from various disciplines to teach us definitive values about what is right and wrong

The trap of relying on experts is described in the following quote by Adam Phillips in *Terrors and Experts*: "When psychoanalysts spend too much time with each other, they start believing in psychoanalysis. They begin to talk knowingly, like members of a religious cult. . . . They forget, in other words, that they are only telling stories about stories, and that all stories are subject to an unknowable multiplicity of interpretations. When psychoanalysis makes too much sense, or makes sense of too much, it turns into exactly the symptom it is trying to cure: defensive knowingness."

To know the unknowable is to become bigger than life. When such ideas are used to develop theories about how to live, we become the people Buddha was talking about when he reminded his followers "Those who grasp at philosophies and views simply wander around the world annoying people."

Knowing things that are presently, and perhaps ultimately, unknowable, or being so definite in our beliefs that we are closed to other possibilities, is a good definition of arrogance. Possessing "the truth" is arrogant, condescending, and distancing. If you are not ready to acknowledge your own arrogance, this idea may sound harsh and judgmental and you may have reacted defensively. If this is the case, as it will be for most people, see if you can nurture yourself into lovingly accepting this part of you.

Without judgment, it is easier to simply acknowledge that we are all arrogant at times. Arrogance is certainly not bad or wrong. It is merely a signal that compassion has taken a back seat to our intellectually preconceived ideas. This dominance of intellect is significantly different from what happens when we are guided by Heart Feelings. The mind is so powerful, however, that it, rather than the heart, usually leads the way.

Humility

Humility is the quality that allows living in the mystery. With humility we are open to holding beliefs loosely enough to receive feedback and change course rather than being slavishly attached to beliefs.

The primary beliefs that keep us from living with humility and from living within the mystery are contained in our beliefs about God. In *Transformations of Myth Through Time*, Joseph Campbell wrote, "We keep thinking of deity as a kind of fact, somewhere; God as fact. God is simply our own notion of something that is transcendence and mystery. The mystery is what's important."

If God is the mystery, then we forsake the mystery (God) when we define it. This is certainly not a new idea. Many ancient civilizations believed that attempts at defining, codifying, or even knowing God would take us away from this unknowable mystery.

At the beginning of the *Tao Te Ching* it says, "The Tao that can be named is not the Tao." Ancient Hebrews believed God's name should not be said aloud, so they wrote it in a way that could not be spoken: YHWH (eventually spoken as Yahweh). God could not be defined or understood— it just was. To be in the mystery was to experience God. Thus God could be experienced, but not known, through our minds. That belief allows for God to be predominately an experience of living with acceptance and awe rather than a being with specific attributes. It brings us closer to ancient wisdom than most commonly held beliefs and its openheartedness results in Fulfilling Connections.

What difference would it make in your life to:

- Live with the humility of knowing that what you believe about unknowable things such as God, reincarnation, morals, or manners is a choice, i.e., "a way" rather than "the way?"
- Not try to get others to believe as you do?
- Have experiences, e.g., dreams, visions, insights, and inner voices, without rigidly holding onto interpretations of those experiences as spirit guides, God, or disembodied spirits?

Letting go of sureness and the desire to predict and control the future allows you to appreciate the perfection and magic of the moment. Transcending your fears of the future leaves you with the experience of wonder. You are more accessible for connection with others. The more you live in that state, the more your life becomes wonder-full.

This is not to suggest that the definite ideas espoused by religions or by the authors of most books or theories should be rejected. That would be like throwing the baby out with the bath water. When you can discern what truly supports connection to your Heart Feelings, you can accept the aspects of ideas that nurture it and reject any parts that foster disconnection. This is the subject of Chapter Eight.

Conventional wisdom views humility as weakness, but in fact it is the greatest power of all. To be humble you must possess the confidence that, whatever happens, you have the ability to create your own sense of well-being. Then you can proceed, even without certainty. Humility is an openness that allows for acceptance of all paths. Letting go of the need to prove, defend, convince, or be in control allows those close to you to gain more trust in your caring.

Humility is the quality that brings appreciation, gratitude, and fulfillment into your life and blesses you with serenity. It is a gift to yourself that relieves you of the worry, tension, and pain that result from a need to prove something. Humility allows you to not take things so seriously, to relax and play with life. You live in the mystery, connected to life and flowing with it, connected to others and flowing with them.

Faith

Humility, living in the mystery, letting go of control, and Fulfilling Connections all depend on one basic issue—faith. Faith is the opposite of control. You know you cannot have control over the future, and you do not have to know or attempt to control the future because it does not matter. You know you can thrive no matter what happens.

Faith is knowing that you are provided with everything you need for your highest good. You may not always get what you want, but you will always get what you need. That kind of faith is cultivated by acknowledging Disconnecting Beliefs and by devoting your energy to ameliorating them. As you walk this path and are better able to bring your beliefs into alignment with your Heart Feelings, you will develop the faith that allows you to let go of the elaborate methods of control that defeat Fulfilling Connections.

Learning About Beliefs

Freeing yourself from the shackles of Disconnecting Beliefs is a step-by-step process that begins with understanding more about both the beliefs driving your fears and the beliefs that bring about Fulfilling Connections.

But dislodging the deeply embedded fears associated with Disconnecting Beliefs usually requires more that merely using your mind's faculties, such as studying, praying, or intoning positive thoughts. Other steps, which might include exploring those beliefs and finally testing them out, are introduced in this chapter, and an exercise for overcoming Disconnecting Beliefs is in the appendix as part of The Fulfilling Connections Process.

Examples of Disconnecting Beliefs are:

- There is not enough of something I need, e.g., love, money (scarcity)
- I do not know how to create my own sense of well-being (dependency)
- The universe is a hostile place (distrust)
- I am responsible for others' well-being; therefore, when others are upset with me, I am bad or wrong
- I am not lovable or adequate; therefore when others reject me, it is because I am inadequate
- I am not smart enough to understand the things that are important for my growth
- I may find out that I am wrong, and if I am wrong I am inadequate
- My personality is fixed, and therefore I am unable to change what needs to be changed
- Whenever I find out something will be painful, I cannot handle it
- I can't handle others' pain (responsibility)
- At my core I am. . . . . (name your poison—rotten, worthless, selfish, unlovable)
- Another person may find out things about me for which I will be rejected

At the bottom of each Disconnecting Belief is the fear of unbearable pain. For example, believing I am not smart enough to understand the things that are important for my growth leads to being rejected and lonely. It is the fear of being in such agony from which we want to protect ourselves. The fear of dreaded pain is almost always the compelling reason for the behaviors that disconnect us from our Heart Feelings.

Examples of Connecting Beliefs are:

- The universe provides an abundance of what I need to create my well-being

- I am capable of creating my own sense of well-being
- The universe is a friendly (or neutral) place
- I am lovable, worthwhile, and adequate
- The sensitive, intellectual, physical, and social parts of myself are wonderful
- The way my body naturally looks is perfect
- There are always very good (important, compelling) reasons for behavior

Connecting Beliefs produce the acceptance and faith that allow your heart to stay open. You may think many of these beliefs are common knowledge. However, by the definition in Chapter Two of "to know," that is, to have an intimate experience of something, they are not. Experiencing Connecting Beliefs in your entire being would mean not just having an intellectual awareness of them, but having them so well-integrated into your psyche that your entire life was a reflection of them.

For example, whenever a Connecting Belief is predominate, you do not take something personally. When others are upset with you, rather than getting defensive, you see their upset as a reflection of their difficulty in keeping their hearts open. Seeing their behavior as a statement about them, not about you, frees you to respond with compassion. For reasons explained later in this chapter, this occurs very infrequently.

Acceptance

An important part of accepting others and ourselves for believing as we do often requires knowing how we got our Disconnecting Beliefs, the purpose they serve, and the results they create. That journey takes us on a fascinating exploration of childhood and culture, as well as into our present relationships.

For example, a most basic, pervasive Disconnecting Belief is that we are wrong, inadequate, unimportant, unlovable, unworthy, or not good enough in how we think, act, or look. Our protections then surround our cavern of self-doubt.

For the most part, self-doubts stemming from the above Disconnecting Beliefs began in infancy, when adults got upset over things we did. We may have been doing natural things like crying, or exploring our bodies, or other parts of our environment. Adults may have gotten angry, made derisive comments, or just become cold and withdrawn their love; but the message was clear—our actions were wrong and, therefore, we were responsible for their upsets.

As children we had no way of knowing that in another home, or in another culture or era, our behavior might not be judged as wrong. So, in our naïveté we formed two beliefs that most devastate our ability to create Fulfilling Connections: First, that when others are upset with something we have done, we are wrong and responsible for the upset; and second, its corollary belief that when we are upset by something others have done, they are wrong and responsible for our feelings.

Guilt thrives on these two Disconnecting Beliefs. They are attempts, usually unconscious, to manipulate others and avoid taking responsibility for our feelings and lives. Escaping from carrying these beliefs into adulthood is almost impossible. For that to happen, we would have to either experience someone taking responsibility for his or her feelings, or possess the wisdom to not take personally the critical judgments of others.

For the former to occur someone would have reacted to his or her upset by taking responsibility for his or her feelings with an intent to learn. He or she would have been curious, and this contemplative attitude would have been reflected in questions like: "I wonder why I'm getting so upset?"; "What are the fears and beliefs of mine that are getting touched off right now?"; "I wonder what's going on with you and why you're behaving as you are?"; or "I wonder what there is to learn from this upset?" How often do you remember anything like the above happening?

For infants not to take the judgments of others personally, they would have to look up into the eyes of an important person who was upset and think, "It's not that I'm unlovable, it's that you're having trouble loving me right now." That is always the truth when someone is upset with us, but since a child cannot be expected to know that, they learn to take others' upsets personally. Can you relate to that?

Once we believe we are responsible for another person's upsets, it follows that they are responsible and wrong when we are upset. For most people, blaming others for our feelings is a favorite pastime. Examples include: "You make me sick" or "You're really upsetting me."

Learning about my core Disconnecting Belief that I could not create my own sense of well-being began with looking into my childhood. My mom was a concerned and dedicated parent, determined to do a good job and raise her kids with love. She read many books on parenting and dedicated her life to her family. However, without anything else compelling in her life and a relationship with my dad that could be described as polite at best, she always hovered close at hand, making sure I never suffered any upsets.

If I was unhappy, she was there to solve my problem, usually even before I asked. In her attempts to be a good mom, she couldn't do enough for me. But not allowing me to struggle and learn to resolve my difficulties and create my own sense of well-being stunted my maturity and created in me a dependent relationship with her. I believed that I needed her to feel happy or even just okay, and my dependency gave her a sense of meaning and worth. That was my first co-dependent relationship.

Growing up, I had many conflicting feelings. Feeling uncomfortable away from home, I wanted to spend lots of time there; but at the same time I began pulling away from Mom. I often felt irritated with her and resisted her attempts to be close with me. I felt guilty feeling this way because she was always so cheerful, interested, and supportive.

As I grew up I transferred my dependency from Mom to sports. In junior high, whenever I was bored or at loose ends, there was a game to play, listen to, watch on TV, or attend. Later, in high school and college, women and sex were added to my repertoire of ways to make myself feel good, if only temporarily. As an adult, success and adulation in my career became new ways to try and get good feelings and affirm that I was okay.

I was miserable when I was not in the activities that temporarily filled my emptiness. I desperately clung to these activities, but in all situations, especially in love relationships, my overwhelming fear of loss led to all kinds of manipulative behavior.

Feeling dependent left me feeling needy, like a child. My deep emptiness would have been evident to anyone who wanted to see it, but no one did. As I stated in Chapter One, even though I became successful and competent in the outside world, inside I felt weak and like I was a fraud.

I was scared to look inside because I believed there was nothing there. For most of my life, I could not admit my nagging self-doubts to myself, let alone others. I never would go into therapy because I was afraid the therapist would see how empty I was. Since I believed that there was nothing to be done about my emptiness, I was stuck. I was fearful that if my secret was revealed, anyone I was with would leave me and I would end up isolated and lonely.

The disintegration of my marriage was the catalyst that led me into therapy. My therapist gently helped me confront and understand why my belief that I was empty was erroneous. I realized that to experience real joy and satisfaction from work, sex, love, and sports, I had to break my dependence upon them. That would necessitate learning how to create my own sense of well-being. My therapist helped me build some of the self-confidence I needed to begin a new life, even if it meant being alone, and to take the next steps toward resolving my imagined emptiness.

In therapy I realized that, even though my beliefs were attempts to protect myself from what I feared would be devastating losses, I was enslaved by them, and that brought about an unhappiness of its own. I couldn't risk letting go of my attempts to control Margie because I was convinced it was the only way to avoid my worst fears.

Fears of unbearable pain exerted a powerful grip that kept me reacting in ways that could never satisfy my deepest needs and wants. Yet I felt powerless to change them. Although I dreamed of a better life, a more fulfilling job, and a more loving relationship, avoiding my fears dominated my life.

Testing Out Disconnecting Beliefs

As previously stated, although it is possible to change a belief by making an intellectual decision to change it, deeply engrained beliefs rarely respond to that kind of effort. For example, telling yourself you are adequate, after years of experiences have convinced you otherwise, is highly unlikely to work.

The most productive way to change deep-seated beliefs is by facing them and proving to yourself they are false. When you believe you are inadequate sexually or intellectually, or you cannot earn enough money to take care of yourself, or you cannot speak in public, the effective way to change these beliefs is to meet them head on and test them out.

When you do something successfully, you will know you really are capable of accomplishing it. When you know you can fail and still thrive, you will not fear failure. When you learn you can feel your deep pain and joy and still thrive, you will not fear your emotions. By your willingness to be more of the person you really are, you will allow yourself to be openhearted and thus feel like your own hero more of the time.

Testing out Disconnecting Beliefs is a uniquely personal journey up a mountain toward the pinnacle of enlightenment I believe we will never reach. Enlightenment is often thought of as being so free of Disconnecting Beliefs that we can be open and unconditionally loving all the time. Since I do not personally know (as opposed to reading about or interacting with the public persona of a person) of anyone living in this world who has achieved that kind of perfection, I choose to believe enlightenment is an ideal state toward which we can strive and feel proud of any movement that takes us closer to it.

For me, the most difficult confrontation during the year prior to my move was how much I depended on Margie, and sex, for my sense of well-being. Margie had been the socket I could plug into for answers to just about everything. Whenever I felt anxious, bored, depressed, or unsure, Margie had always been there trying to make me feel better by offering everything from comforting aphorisms, to advice, to her body.

When Margie, feeling my ever-increasing pull to spend time together and to have sex, decided that she needed some space, that shoved me into confronting my dependence on women to be my emotional caretakers. Margie didn't want a formal separation but suggested that we continue to live together, sleep in separate bedrooms, and have little to do with each other emotionally as well as physically.

That bombshell sent me into my next therapy session swimming in a sea of fear and self-doubt. I told my therapist what Margie had decided, sat back, and sighed, "What do you think I should do?"

He responded sympathetically, "I wish I could give you some simple ideas that would make your pain immediately disappear, but I can't. I take back what I just said; even if I could wave a magic wand, I wouldn't. I don't believe that either protecting you from your pain, or giving you advice is what you need.

"I want to help you discover how to trust your inner knowing. That will be truly empowering. When connected to your essence, what you should do will become clear and the results will be satisfying. Until that time we can explore what's creating your unhappiness and I'll suggest some reading material that will help you."

Over the next few months I worked diligently on myself. I read books, talked with friends about the concepts I was learning, and came into each therapy session ready with feelings and issues I wanted to learn more about. Things really started to fall into place when I uncovered the core belief that I couldn't create my own sense of well-being. This unconscious belief of my inability to create my own joy had been running my life, and it was responsible for much of the fear that kept me disconnected from my heart and produced a great deal of my controlling behavior.

The terror of losing the relationship was so great that I needed somehow to keep Margie hooked in. Irritation and anger were my weapons of choice to maintain some kind of control. They worked because my upsets activated her belief that she was somehow responsible for my well-being.

As long as she believed it was her responsibility to make me feel better, and that if I was not being loving toward her she was doing something wrong, I had her. It was part our system, the unconscious dance that we equally created. Now, as my illusion of control began shattering, I was looking and learning with new eyes.

I discovered that without knowing how to connect to my inner knowing about what I wanted and needed to feel good, I had focused on my connection to Margie. After all, when we were together I felt good and calm. Most other times I felt out of sorts and preoccupied with what Margie was doing, afraid I would lose her, and wanting to be spending time with her. My fear disconnected me from my heart.

Although our mutual sexual experience was one of the few times that I experienced my compassion, joy, playfulness, and serenity, after much deliberation I realized that to heal the place in me that relied on sex as a way to connect I needed to give up sex for a while. During that time I would try to develop a wider variety of ways to feel good about myself. The thought terrified me.

I had thought about sex constantly since I was a teenager. I would have liked to make love every day if Margie had been willing. When she began pulling away sexually, I began thinking about having sex with anything that wore a skirt. Instead, I chose to go cold turkey and deal with, rather than act on, the feelings that were associated with my sexuality. It was like an alcoholic promising to give up alcohol.

When I mentioned to a few of my friends that I was going to become celibate, they thought I was crazy. Thankfully, by that time I was in a men's group. In sharing my sexual thoughts, feelings, and difficulties, I received understanding and support for my decision. In fact, two other men made the same commitment. We were a great support for each other during the times between group meetings.

After being in therapy for a year, I moved to Aspen and my self-confrontations accelerated. Giving up sex was a major test, but an even bigger one appeared. In August I met Georgia at a conference. We had a whirlwind three-day romance before she left to return home. Our feelings for each other blossomed over the phone with conversations lasting into the wee hours of the morning. She knew of my commitment to celibacy and, since she was dealing with her own sexual issues, felt very comfortable with that limitation. By December we had decided that she would return to Aspen and stay in my guest bedroom.

As the days turned into weeks, I knew that although I felt great in passing my own test of no sex, I was ready for a deeper commitment. I felt ready for a relationship that included the intimacy of affection and shared emotional feelings. Georgia didn't feel she was ready for that. In addition, she gently suggested that I might not be ready as well. I scoffed at that notion, but was comfortable in maintaining the relationship at its present level.

I was not as successful as I had hoped at keeping my heart open without affection and emotional feelings being present. The relationship began to decline, and within a month Georgia decided that she should return home.

As we rode to the airport, Georgia broke our silence when she said, "Don't be sad. Everything is going to be just fine."

I countered, half jokingly, "You know, Georgia, I'm sure that by God's plan that's true. I'm just upset that my plan isn't working."

One night, months later, as I lay in bed, I thought of that comment and realized the arrogance of thinking that I could always know what was right for myself. I looked up toward the heavens and wondered if there was a God who was enjoying giving me another lesson in humility.

I knew that the process of learning to keep my heart open, no matter what was happening, would keep my feet to the fire. I knew that this was a profound notion, and I had some doubts about whether I was up to the challenge. I considered the possibility that, "Although I might always have some doubts, maybe the journey was in just feeling that I was making some headway." That thought felt right and comforted me as it lulled me to sleep.

As I became more successful in relating to women without thoughts of love or sex pressing at the front of my head and at the fly of my jeans, my relationships became a whole new experience. I discovered friendship. I could talk to and get to know a woman without trying to maneuver her into bed.

Women opened up to me like never before and I felt comfortable being thought of as "one of the girls." I liked being a friend, whether it was for one night or longer. I felt like I was expressing a higher part of myself. Knowing that I was being genuine left me feeling better about myself than I had ever felt before. And now, for the first time since I felt the stirring of sexual desire as an adolescent, I felt in charge of my sexuality rather than my sexuality running me.

Intimacy had taken on an entirely different meaning. It was no longer something by which I needed to prove my worth. I knew I would have both emotional and sexual intimacy when it felt right. That would be when I felt connected to my heart and was with a woman who was connected to her heart.

Surprisingly, some of my most important lessons about creating my sense of well-being came from skiing. I had come to Aspen determined to become a better skier. I worked hard and braved many miserably cold days to improve. But one day as Lee and I were talking about having fun, I realized that I wasn't having fun skiing. "What's missing?" I asked. "What do you get out of skiing?"

Lee thought for a moment and said, "You know, I used to be obsessed with my technique just like you. But one day I was skiing by myself. It was a glorious, crystal clear, sparkling day and I got into just connecting with all of nature's grandeur and perfection—the majesty of the mountains, the purity of the snow, the deep blue of the sky. It was a spiritual experience. Since then, no matter what the technical level of my skiing, I enjoy nothing more than my time on the slopes."

The next day I had a leisurely breakfast, got to the mountain at 10:00 a.m. instead of my usual 8:30, and skied with an entirely different orientation. It was sensational. At the end of the day when I met Lee in the Jacuzzi, I was beaming.

"You know," I said, hardly able to contain my excitement, "today I learned how skiing alone can be very satisfying. But I also realized that when you and I ski together, it's also fun and satisfying because of our rides together up the chair lift, our lunches on the mountain, and our stopping and chatting during our runs. I'm really excited by what a difference it would make anytime I go skiing with another person if I made connecting with that person the primary reason I was out on the slopes."

Skiing became one of my favorite ways to connect deeply to myself and to others. When I was connected in this way, my sense of well-being soared. I eagerly looked forward to skiing dates as times when I could spend time with friends without the usual distractions of life. Even the days when the chair lift got stuck and we dangled high above the ground were opportunities to connect, and so became enjoyable.

One day while having lunch at Ruthie's restaurant, watching the skiers glide downhill, and greeting friend after friend, I thought, "I know many of my old friends would never believe this, but when I connect with myself, nature, and my friends, skiing is just as good as having sex. Wow, what a concept! I better keep this one just between Lee and myself."

Learning to create my own sense of well-being allowed for a freedom I had never imagined possible. Lee and I developed a relationship that incorporated many wonderful aspects of true friendship. We established a deep emotional and spiritual bond without imposing any restrictions on the other.

This was illustrated one Fourth of July when we were cruising Main Street during the holiday parade. At noon, under a cloudless cerulean sky, began the corny, yet always wonderful, hometown extravaganza featuring a procession of dogs wearing western bandannas, a cavalcade of floats and marching bands, and the volunteer fire department driving their engines while throwing candy to the kids.

Everyone was having a great time, and it was people at their best. Lee and I wanted to soak up every connection we could make. As we wove through the crowd, we stopped every few feet to talk with friends. We were totally in our element, having great fun enjoying ourselves and enjoying each other.

We'd gotten half way up Main Street when the float of the Aspen Kayak School stopped in front of us. Lee spotted it and spontaneously began running toward the float, yelling to me, "I want to ride in the kayak. I'll catch up with you later." As Lee climbed into the kayak on top of the float and began laughing with his kayaking buddies and kibitzing with friends on the sidewalk, I was delighted and continued my journey.

Hours later we rendezvoused near the end of the parade route. We shared our experiences as we walked toward The Cantina restaurant for some refreshments. I talked about how different it felt being able to support someone making a spontaneous decision to change plans. I said, "In the past, if Margie had done something like that, I would have been upset. When we got back together, to teach her a lesson to never break an agreement or disappoint me, I probably would have been cold and withdrawn. It would have been an awful reunion. Instead, you and I just pick up where we leave off and continue having a wonderful time."

Lee smiled, "You know, if I ever thought that something like that would be really difficult for you, we'd talk about it. But knowing you'll have a great time whether I'm there or not really frees me. I love that part of our relationship. Do you think it's possible to have that kind of freedom in a committed relationship with a woman?"

"Hmmm," I replied, "I don't know, but I sure hope so."

Later that evening in the crystal clear altitude of 8,000 feet, the vivid colors of the fireworks display and sparkling lights exploding in concert with my favorite selections of classical music moved me to tears. That was the dessert course for the most incredible holiday celebration I had ever had.

Things weren't always rosy for Lee and me. At times, "stuff" came up, but we knew that no matter what time of the day or what we were doing, we would always be there for each other. One day, after an upsetting telephone conversation with Margie, I rode my bike to Lee's frame shop.

Lee immediately sensed something was wrong. "Hey, bud, you look like you could use a talk. Jerry can watch the shop—how about you and I going for a walk?"

We started down the Rio Grande Trail toward the river. "What's going on?" Lee asked.

"I just had an awful interaction with Margie. It's been months since we last talked and I just felt like checking in to see how she was doing. For a while things went really well. She shared stuff she was learning about astral travel that in the past would have sent me into orbit. This time I was able to put into practice things you and I had been talking about. Instead of trying to talk her out of her experience, I focused on finding out what the experience meant to her.

"It was magical. We were having a great talk until I said something about how I was learning not to get hooked into proving something was right or wrong and what a difference that was making in our interactions. Out of the blue, she says, 'I'm feeling uncomfortable right now. It feels like you're pulling on me.'

"Well, I lost it. I was just expressing my excitement and she drops that same old crap on me. You know, sometimes I think she's just nuts. She's so damn unappreciative." I looked to Lee for approval of my evaluation of Margie. I didn't get it.

"Seems like you're in some pain about that," Lee gently suggested.

With that, my anger drained, my body lost some of its rigidity, and I confessed, "Yeah, I feel she's always so defensive that she doesn't really see me. She thinks of me as such a bad guy, like I'm only after something for myself. She's even called me selfish and narcissistic. It feels lousy."

We had reached the river and Lee suggested we wade out to a big flat rock that lay newly exposed from the retreating winter's thaw. Sitting in the middle of the river in the bright June sun with my best friend at my side felt like heaven. And then he dropped the "Lee-shell": "Do you want some feedback?" he asked.

"Sure, I think," I said with a half-hearted attempt at some humor.

"Well, I don't think Margie is crazy. Your conscious intent may not have been to get something from her, but my guess is that there was a part of you that wanted something. Can you think of anything else that may have been going on for you?"

I thought for a minute and then said sheepishly, "I was feeling a little lonely and I guess I wanted to connect with her." After another pause I continued, "I also wanted her to know how well I'm doing. I guess her approval is still important to me." After a very brief pause, I added, "But I really was interested in finding out about her."

"I'm sure all those things are true," Lee said, "but she only picked up on the part that felt invasive. You know that setting boundaries has been an issue for her. But what does that tap into for you?"

"I guess it's hard for me to cop to all the different parts of myself. I still get hooked into the belief that I'm wrong if my intentions are not strictly honorable. And I guess I haven't made it okay to be selfish at times. But I am."

"I know," said Lee, "and I love you anyway." We reached out and hugged each other.

We continued chatting on our river oasis for a while longer before it was time to go. When we stood up Lee asked, "How are you feeling?"

"Much better," I replied. As I looked at him I shook my head in gratitude for this man who, by modeling the ability to live in his heart rather than his head, had opened me to so many gifts that I might never have known.

After nearly five years in Aspen, I realized what I wanted to do with the rest of my life could not be done from within the community of that cloistered oasis. The hardest part of that decision was leaving my best friend. As I stood on the balcony that last afternoon looking out at Aspen Mountain, the swell in my heart overflowed onto my cheeks. The afternoon rain shower had left one of those intense Rocky Mountain rainbows as its legacy. I chuckled to myself as I recanted the often-used phrase, "No rain, no rainbows."

I thought, "What a trip this has been." Things that had happened that had brought me to this moment flashed through my mind: separating from Margie, celibacy, moving to a new town, meeting Georgia, my friendship with Lee, and the plethora of feelings that I allowed myself to feel—the terror and serenity, the anger and joy. "All of that," I thought, "has merely been grist for the mill, opportunities to learn and grow—gifts from Spirit."

Although I felt refreshed and ready to go home, there were some lingering disquieting thoughts that surfaced. "I know I haven't reached the Emerald City. This is merely a plateau before continuing to climb the infinite mountain. I've proven I can be happy alone, but I know that the challenges that come only in intimate relationships are waiting in my future."

Lee joined me on the balcony. He always had a way of turning up at the right time. I shared what I had been thinking and feeling. When I finished, we hugged in a way that only two deeply connected friends could.

As we looked skyward we were awed as a magnificent double rainbow appeared. I said sheepishly, "Tell me the truth," as if Lee had ever not been truthful with me. "You know how I've always put down as New Age nonsense the idea that there are no coincidences. What do you think?"

Lee laughed, "I don't know and I don't give a shit. Remember what grandma said at the end of the movie *Parenthood*—'You can live life on a merry-go-round or on a roller coaster.' We're on the roller coaster, bud, and it's a great ride. Let's get going or you'll miss your plane."

As I reached for my bags, I quipped, "Let's hope the ride I'm about to take is a merry-go-round!" I thought of what Lee had brought to my life and choking back the tears as I gave him a hug, kissed him on the cheek and said, "Thanks, bro."

Chapter Four

Relationships, Our Most Profound Teachers

In the safe place that a warm relationship provides, one can allow the more divergent parts of one's personality to emerge—including one's anger—and once those are acknowledged and assimilated, there's just "more of me there" to bring into that relationship and others. Conversely, of course, when I know that only a very narrow version of myself will find acceptance (the "nice and kind" parts, for example), I feel defeated before I even begin to unfold.

—Carol Lee Flinders, *At the Root of This Longing: Reconciling a Spiritual Hunger and a Feminist Thirst*

While staying connected to one's heart when alone is not easy, being in a relationship presents an even greater challenge. Since important relationships touch our deepest fears and wounds, staying heart connected and feeling like our own hero is rare. Therefore, learning about Heart Feelings and disconnected behaviors can become a very important, although usually unrecognized, reason to be married, to have children, and to be in business. Fulfilling Connections in all of these areas will be explored independently in subsequent chapters.

Even those inspirational role models whose legacy revealed to us the power of an open heart, such as Jesus, Buddha, or Mother Theresa, didn't always model an openness in their close personal relationships. They never had to deal with a mate who was unaffectionate or noncommunicative, or a child who was experimenting with drugs, smoking, or sex. They never had to find a career that was both satisfying and brought in enough money to support a family. They never had to deal with an employee who had seniority but was incompetent and unproductive. And many statesmen and spiritual leaders, such as Gandhi, whose lives were exemplary in meeting difficulties in the outside world with an open heart did not demonstrate this ability in their personal lives.

On the other hand, responding to disconnected behaviors with disconnected behaviors is well documented. Unfortunately, our history is a chronicle of people behaving in ways that reflect disconnection from their hearts, some using power to dominate and control, and others responding passively. But you don't have to read about this in history books. Just turn on your television set. News stories, legislative sessions, and most dramas and soap operas clearly illustrate the power plays and the negative responses that reflect a disconnection from heart.

Part of the excitement and challenge of the journey toward becoming powerful and creating Fulfilling Connections lies in being a pioneer of what is a truly uncommon way of being. Though a lofty ideal, it is one well worth striving for. Staying open when others are not is like rising out of the muck and mire of common responses and walking on water. That's real power.

An inspiring contemporary example of the power of staying connected to one's heart when another person is not is described in the book *Not By The Sword* by Kathryn Watterson. The book relates the true story of Rabbi Michael Weisser and his relationship with Larry Trapp, Grand Dragon of the White Knights of the Ku Klux Klan of Nebraska. In the book, Rabbi Weisser recounts that, the day he and his family moved into their new home, he received the first of many threatening calls from Larry Trapp: "You will be sorry you ever moved into 5810 Randolph Street, Jew boy!"

Trapp was a man the FBI and local police considered armed and dangerous. For years, he had led a campaign of terror in Lincoln, Nebraska. He was an angry and hate-filled person. He lived holed up in a small apartment packed with enough weapons to blow up a small city.

Trapp had the city paralyzed with fear. Accustomed to inspiring fear in others, Trapp was caught off guard when Rabbi Weisser and his wife refused to be intimidated. Instead, the Rabbi kept making offers of friendship to Trapp. Trapp at first refused and even increased his reign of terror.

But Rabbi Weisser never closed his heart, and he continued to reach out with love. Eventually his persistence broke through Trapp's armor and a friendship began. Finally, Trapp shocked everyone, including himself, by resigning from the KKK and breaking his ties with other national neo-Nazi and white supremacist leaders.

"They showed me such love that I couldn't help but love them back . . . ," Trapp later said. Larry Trapp spent the rest of his life in service to others.

A place to begin learning about staying more connected to your heart in relationships can be by taking a look at the disconnected feelings and behaviors that arise when you are upset with another person. This assumes your willingness to learn about what you are now doing, or have done in the past, that is not loving or nurturing to yourself and to others, especially at times when things do not go as you like.

You may not have previously linked these disconnected feelings and behavior with the negative consequences that they create. This new way of thinking, however, is illuminating, sometimes shocking, and often sobering. It requires the courage to acknowledge:

- Responsibility for your part in the situations that are making you unhappy
- A pervasive need for control and power
- The pain that others feel when they are at the other end of your behavior
- The unhappiness that you inflict on yourself

This is what we all want to deny. We want to see ourselves as good and loving people, and we are. But we also have that shadow side and acknowledging it usually requires a safe place. The idea of an inner learning sanctuary was introduced in Chapter Two. Creating a relationship sanctuary is the focus of this chapter.

Relationship Sanctuary

For most people, "relationship sanctuary" may seem like an oxymoron. A dictionary definition of sanctuary is "a place of refuge and protection," "a refuge from turmoil and strife." A sanctuary is typically found in the isolation of a closed room, a favorite spot in nature, or by listening to music on headphones. Around other people we are often on edge, worried about what others will think and do if they are offended or disappointed.

In a relationship sanctuary we feel safe in knowing that we can express ourselves with a reasonable expectation of not being criticized or rejected. Imagine being at home, at work, or at a community gathering and not feeling afraid to express unusual ideas or experiences you are having, and to feel confident you have the freedom to make a mistake or fail and not lose the support of those around you. Put aside your skepticism and let that idea sink in.

For the dream of a relationship sanctuary to become real, it must resist the tendency to develop a relationship form that is defined by rigid rules and expectations. Instead, by creating a context for respectfully dealing with differences and accommodating change, a relationship can assume a fluid form, one that allows for changing shapes in both individuals and the institution itself.

Most of the forms within which we interact, such as religion, marriage, business, and culture, do not have a context that allows for fluidity. As a result, a vehicle that may promise liberation, often becomes a prison. In a relationship sanctuary, the form does not limit the free expression of its members as long as the rights of others are not infringed upon. An environment that encourages people to take risks with thoughts and behavior that are "outside the box" is true freedom. Without that freedom, we lose the knowledge of who we really are and become the form: for example, American, black, Jewish, female, male, a doctor, Christian.

Take a look at the forms in which you live. Are people encouraged to try new ideas and behavior without negative consequences being imposed? What are the limits beyond which you cannot go without risking your emotional safety, or even your sense of belonging? Does your workplace culture require you to leave your personal self at the door? Does your marriage say you cannot spend a week by yourself or develop a friendship with a person of the opposite sex? Does your religion demand allegiance to a defined set of beliefs? Do the forms in which you are living feel like a sanctuary?

When a relationship is a true refuge, all of us is welcome—our feelings, thoughts, fears, talents, hopes, and dreams. It is then a place where our soul is not intruded upon. The more we feel all of ourselves being honored, the greater the value of the relationship. It becomes a place to which we want to return more and more often. A relationship sanctuary feels like home – perhaps not the one we grew up in, but the one for which we have deeply longed.

In a relationship sanctuary, the parts of ourselves we have banished to the shadows can be exposed, tended to, accepted, celebrated, and healed. Heart Feelings are nurtured and the warmth of Fulfilling Connections produce a sharp contrast to the iciness and emptiness that follow the "right doing and wrong doing" of disconnected feelings and behavior. To create a relationship sanctuary, we have to know that we can keep our hearts open and:

- Teach our kids to be responsible
- Create profitable businesses and work groups that function effectively
- Produce successful and winning teams
- Have loving relationships with our mate without losing ourselves
- Set and enforce standards

Although no one lives in a perfect sanctuary, we can always be in the process of making our relationships into better ones. To determine where we can do better in creating such a sanctuary, the most telling question we must face is "Do those around us feel cared about and loved?" This is a very different question than "Do those around us know that we care for and love them?"

Many of us would like to believe that we can consistently respond uncaringly and others will feel cared about. But it doesn't work that way. Being angry when someone is late does not communicate that we are worried. Attempting to restrain someone from doing something that upsets or frightens us does not translate as love. Punishing people who have broken rules or failed to keep their commitments does not demonstrate that we care about them.

People may know somewhere inside themselves that we care about them and yet not feel cared about unless they feel the safety of knowing that they will be treated respectfully, especially when they do something that upsets us. Otherwise, our love is conditional, based on others never doing anything that goes against something we judge as wrong or bad.

We must ask ourselves, "Does our response to a difficulty let others know they are cared about and loved?" A heart-connected response communicates all those things. On the other hand, disconnected responses communicate that, in that moment, something, such as teaching a lesson or making a point, is more important than their feelings or needs. Feeling deeply cared about requires a consistency in caring responses.

Since only a "God" is capable of consistently giving unconditional love, this is an area in which we all struggle. Mere mortals cannot stay connected to their Heart Feelings all the time. When deep fears are activated we all lose our heart connection. But the good news is that even when we lose it, caring can be communicated in another way. We can learn to better recognize when we have treated another person in an unloving manner, and can clean up the wounds we have inflicted. This is done by:

- Acknowledging that our actions were unloving
- Communicating that we care about the fact that the other person has been hurt
- Making a sincere effort to heal whatever has gotten in the way of a heart-connected response

When we don't clean up the mess created by our unloving behavior, wounds fester, apologies become meaningless, and walls of protection and distrust build.

Trust in a Relationship Sanctuary

In the thriving realm of a relationship sanctuary, trust is a treasured asset. A high level of trust translates into palpable feelings of serenity, excitement, passion and optimism. These are the feelings that usually accompany the beginning of life in a new community, such as when moving to a town, starting a new job, falling in love, or bringing a baby into the world. But as disconnecting interactions erode trust, these feelings cannot be maintained. Without trust, the vitality, creativity, productivity, and joy is drained from participants.

Attempting to relate in a sea of distrust is like trying to swim through a stream that is being polluted with more and more debris. Low trust spawns adversarial relationships that must slosh through the muck and mire of defensiveness, cynicism, and indifference. Stalemates, resistance, rebellion, boredom, arguments, and power struggles weave a picture that bears little resemblance to the tapestry that existed before trust was eroded.

As our society becomes more complex, trust becomes more and more important. Yet many people believe that trust should be added to the list of endangered species. Without trust, people withhold or distort the truth and communication breaks down. Problems mount and solutions remain more and more outside of our individual or collective capabilities. Whether we are trying to make our family life satisfying, our career successful, or our world more peaceful, it takes more and more effort at the same time as we experience an increasing number of failures.

The following is a brief description of the devastation that low trust wreaks on relationships:

- Feeling in love with our mate suffers when we do not trust that we will be respected for our different styles

- Families suffer when kids believe they will not be respected if they tell their parents the truth, and parents do not trust that their children are telling them the truth
- Businesses suffer when labor and management do not trust that the other cares
- Education suffers when students do not trust that their teachers care about them more than the subject matter they are being taught, and teachers do not trust that students will work hard unless they are threatened
- Effective communities cannot occur when people do not trust their politicians, doctors, lawyers, auto mechanics, or law enforcement officers

Distrust of others almost always translates to a belief that we will not be treated respectfully. "I don't trust you" then means "I don't believe that you will treat me respectfully." How different would your life be if you believed that your neighbors, bosses, employees, and loved ones would treat you respectfully? How different would your relationships with others be if they believed that you would treat them more respectfully? What difference would it make if you believed that you would treat yourself more respectfully?

Although most people recognize trust as an important issue, their focus is almost always away from themselves. "I don't trust you!" makes another person wrong. It does not contain Heart Feelings or Heart Learning and only serves to perpetuate alienation. When we look at trust with an open heart, the question moves from outside oneself, "Can I trust you?" to inside oneself, "Am I trustworthy (a person worthy of trust)?" "How am I being disrespectful to myself and others?" opens the door for learning more about respect and thereby building greater trust in all our relationships.

Respect in a Relationship Sanctuary

When trust is abundant, respect is the coin of the realm. Respect is a universally acclaimed value. One dictionary definition of respect is "to treat something as sacred." Another dictionary definition is "The behavior that nurtures the well-being of oneself and others." Although the definitions may seem clear, what it means to be respectful is subject to many interpretations.

Overcoming some of the confusion can be accomplished by focusing on the behavior that flows naturally from an open heart. With an open heart each person is seen as sacred and treated with the behavior accorded a Divine being. Respectful behavior honors us by understanding that first, we are each a unique expression of the Divine; and second, given our fears and Disconnected Beliefs, we are always doing the best we can. Knowing this, we do not try to change others, even when their choices result in difficult feelings or situations for us, for them, or for others. That is the unconditional acceptance of love.

As previously mentioned, even with the best of intentions, the fears and Disconnected Beliefs that are part of the package of being human sometimes get in the way of expressing that kind of acceptance. However, by holding respectful behavior as our goal and working to remove whatever blocks keep us from it, we can always be moving toward his ideal.

For respect to be given more than lip service, it must be an operating principle in each of our relationships, especially in the face of disagreement. For this to occur, two ideas radically different from traditional thinking must be integrated into our relationships: First, disrespectful behavior can never be justified; and second, respectful behavior must be held as important as accomplishing our goals.

Justifying disrespectful behavior leaves us stuck in the knee-jerk responses that follow the legacy of traditional thinking like: "An eye for an eye and a tooth for a tooth," "This is for your own good," or "This hurts me more than it does you." Criminals are treated inhumanely, mates rage at each other, children are hit, and employees are given short shrift.

Putting a big red negative line through a circle labeled Disrespectful Behavior forces us to think outside the box of common knowledge. When there is never a justifiable rationale for disrespectful behavior, we must pause and consider responses that preserve both our integrity and that of others. This does not condone the disrespectful behavior of others, and it does not mean turning the other cheek and allowing ourselves to be continually disrespected. It is thinking of a much deeper order. It requires learning not only what it means to consider other people, but also how to take care of ourselves in a loving way.

In general, when disrespectful behavior is justified, we do not open to learning. We react and then, believing that the other person deserved to get what was coming to them, we retreat in self-righteousness. When another person's behavior hurts us emotionally or physically, or another person is involved in activities that may be harmful to them and to us, openness to learning addresses such formidable questions as:

- What was the feeling that caused your heart to close?

- What are the negative consequences of your actions on your relationship and yourself?
- If fear and Disconnecting Beliefs weren't present and your heart was open, what would you have felt and how would you have responded? [This is really difficult. To fully understand it you have to imagine what would be the response of a good friend who was not feeling threatened by the situation.]
- What are the positive results to yourself and your relationship of keeping your heart open?
- What do you fear happening if you keep your heart open?
- What are the beliefs responsible for this fear?
- What must you do to resolve this fear?

Applying these questions to specific situations with mates, children, and people at work will be addressed in Chapters Five through Seven.

Making respectful behavior as important as tasks and goals is a radical paradigm shift. It moves us away from the traditional "either/or" thinking, which sees only two alternatives, to the visionary "both/and" thinking, which values the wisdom and possibilities of accomplishing multiple goals simultaneously. In the business world, rather than profits being the primary goal, both/and thinking sets its sights on a "double or triple bottom line." Although the inclusive thinking of both/and may seem like common sense, deeper examination will illuminate how rarely it is practiced and the significant difference it makes when incorporated into our lives.

In building a successful business, teaching a lesson, getting a job done, or winning a game, the means used to accomplish these tasks and goals are rarely given equal importance with the ends themselves. Without such a conscious and dedicated commitment, the means often lapse into disrespectful behavior. For example, parents often teach their children how to be careful, be respectful, have good manners, be responsible, and so on, in ways that are often disrespectful to the child.

When neither a heart connection nor tasks can be compromised, new ways must often be found to accomplish our tasks. When this idea was introduced to a junior high school vice-principal, he said, "Are you saying we can't discipline?" The answer was, "No, but ways to discipline must be found that do not compromise anyone's integrity."

Consider the long-term consequences to a business when employees, customers, or the environment are not respected. Consider the long-term consequences to yourself when your own behavior has been disrespectful to your emotional or physical well-being. Almost all relationship breakdowns, depression, deteriorating health, and business and career failures result from a history of disrespect and distrust. Only when we recognize the enormous price that is paid when people or the environment are disrespected will we be open to adopting a new paradigm in our organizations and families. An example of how this idea might be applied in a business setting is included in Chapter Seven.

Learning About Respectful Behavior

Learning about respectful behavior may prove more challenging than you might imagine. The following list compares some specific respectful and disrespectful behaviors:

Respectful Behavior	*Disrespectful Behavior*
Honoring. Being aware of and considering other people's boundaries—their right not to have anything done to them that they do not want done, or that violates their sensitivities.	*Manipulation.* Attempting to control people and things. Not considering what others want, think, or feel, thus violating their physical and/or emotional boundaries.
Accepting. Appreciating differences by valuing and supporting the choices and feelings of others.	*Punishing.* Imposing or threatening negative consequences—hitting, yelling, or silence when upset with another.
Empathetic Feedback. Feedback that acknowledges and understands the feelings of others. It follows from knowing that all behavior is motivated by important reasons.	*Criticizing/Judging.* Making others wrong for their thoughts, feelings, actions, or words. Communicating that another person is stupid, a jerk, crazy, weird, etc.
Being Inclusive. Inviting others to participate in discussions and decisions about things that affect them.	*Being Unavailable.* Making other things more important than being fully present and really hearing another.
Cooperation. Considering and valuing each person's thoughts and feelings when working on tasks and goals.	*Egotistical Competition.* Interactions where there is a need to prove something or win, at the expense of another.
Faith. Maintaining one's caring while allowing others to solve their own problems, especially in the face of difficulties.	*Caretaking.* Enabling dependency by taking responsibility for others and continuing to do things for them that they are capable of doing for themselves.
Humility. Remaining unattached to beliefs. Having strong ideas but holding them lightly enough to remain open and flexible.	*Unsolicited Sharing.* Expressing feelings or pushing information and advice that has not been asked for and is not wanted.
Open to Learning. Desiring to learn about oneself and others when differences occur. Having faith that solutions which do not compromise anyone's integrity emerge from exploration and learning.	*Arguing/Debating/Persuading.* Attempts to win, get one's way, be right, or prove a point by convincing others to change their beliefs and behavior.

Heart Learning is always respectful. The moment we open ourselves to learning, all disrespectful behavior stops and begins again only when we lose our heart connection.

"Power Over" or "Power With"

Understanding power and its use is essential for becoming personally powerful and creating a relationship sanctuary. Power is neither intrinsically good nor bad: it is merely a force. Our relationship to power manifests when we are in leadership positions. We are all leaders at various times: parents lead families, supervisors lead work teams, teachers lead students, coaches lead athletes, elected officials lead cities and towns. A leader's responsibility is awesome; leaders assume a power that can be used to control and disempower those whom they lead, or to facilitate personal power and Fulfilling Connections. Power becomes an issue whenever differences occur— for example, when expectations are not met, agreements are broken, or disagreements arise over beliefs, opinions, needs, or wants.

It is easy to be a benevolent leader, caring and easy to get along with, as long as things go our way. But when the negative impact of things not going as we would like taps into our fears, our penchant for control takes over. The feeling of helplessness brings back those dreaded childhood feelings of vulnerability and powerlessness. Those feelings are so disturbing that a great deal of our behavior is designed (albeit subconsciously) to deny them and to avoid situations that may provoke them.

Using power to impose our will by making and enforcing decisions about how others should behave, think, and feel is the prevalent model for responding to differences. It is another example of fear triumphing over compassion, and the results of the ensuing adversarial process speak for themselves. It will be referred to as the Power Over model.

Fear and control are integral parts of us and therefore are integral to every institution. Families, religions, business, politics, and education, all operate in systems that actively use power to control others. A Power Over model uses what another fears, or believes they need, to get them to behave – for example, withholding, or threatening to withhold, money, good grades, salvation, a job, approval, sex, or love. The Power Over model is good for building monolithic institutions and power bases, but it is vested in keeping others disempowered, and it is guaranteed to create alienation and separation.

Without connection to heart as an operating principle, institutionalized practices not only do not support knowing our own worth and glory, but also severely limit the success of the institutions themselves. Punctuated by vacillations between control and dependency, our relationships become the source of our greatest disappointments and frustrations. Additionally, using power to control others is the core issue in every form of discrimination, and until it is addressed, efforts to end oppression will be severely limited.

When differences occur, the Power Over model clashes with our genetically programmed push toward freedom and independence. A mother bird gently nudging her chick out of the nest exemplifies how animals honor this drive by preparing and encouraging their young toward freedom. However, in the human world, independence is discouraged and adherence is venerated. The powerlessness of childhood can be interminable and the pain of being shackled excruciating. Although this pain is ameliorated by our capacity to cut ourselves off from painful feelings, it is not hard to imagine a universal mantra being "Someday *I'm* going to be in charge!"

The dependency of childhood, which in the past lasted only until adolescence, now extends well into adulthood. By the time we emerge from our prison of dependency, we carry both repressed painful feelings and a pervasive fear of being dependent again. Our adult life is characterized by being on both sides of the fence, being the controller at times and allowing ourselves to be controlled at other times.

The Power Over model is rooted in the belief that in any situation there are only two positions—"one up" or "one down." The fear of being one down and losing freedom is so great that it overpowers compassion and creates the need to dominate and control. Therefore, the basic intent of using power to protect ourselves from being controlled comes from a fear that we will not be able to hold our own and take care of ourselves. Although people who are successful in getting others to bend to their will are often seen as strong, their fear of being controlled is their "Achilles' heel." In *Escape from Freedom*, renowned psychoanalyst Dr. Erich Fromm cautions us: "The lust for power is not rooted in strength but in weakness."

Threats are an obvious example of trying to be "one up." Attempts to exercise control can also be very subtle, however. We all use indirect means to try to get someone to change and most of us are unaware of how much our life is determined by this powerful drive to exercise control. You can recognize the controlling part of yourself when you:

- Try to convince others to change their beliefs or behavior by using guilt, logic, threats, or any other means to impose your beliefs
- Gather ammunition that supports your beliefs and store it for future battles

- Go over and over conversations in your mind, readying yourself for the real thing
- Are rigidly attached to beliefs about unknowable issues

It is difficult to acknowledge how controlling we are because we do not like to see ourselves in that light. Yet, at times, we are all controlling. Although some people may seem more controlling than others, it is usually just the areas of control that differ, depending on our greatest areas of fear.

Power Over is not, as some people think, a masculine form of power. It is true that for ages men have used their physical and financial power to control others. But, women have used power to control in the areas where they have had power of their own, most notably in child raising and in areas where men might need something from them, such as approval or sex.

A woman withdrawing love from a child, using guilt or her physical strength to enforce her wishes, is no different than a man using his power to enforce his demands. In fact, the home is where we first learn about control and oppression. In the dimension of Power Over, men are not the enemy of women or vice versa. We all suffer from the effects of being oppressed by those in power. Our common enemy is the set of beliefs that create our fears of loss.

The Power Over model is about engaging in a battle to win. It is not about learning, caring, respect, listening, finding the truth, or finding solutions that meet everyone's needs. The Power Over model is responsible for dominating and stagnating every institution, including politics, business, religion, and education. A blatant example is illustrated in our legal system. That system, whose motto extols truth and justice, is often in reality an adversarial system, where winning overpowers the other expressed values.

To some degree, we are all practicing attorneys, using whatever means we have available to win, or at least to not lose. As previously stated, we have been subjected to the Power Over model from our earliest days. We suffered under it and learned skills to survive within it. Now, when we find ourselves in positions of power, we use those skills.

When we fear that the loss of something will be intolerable, trying to exercise control to prevent that loss is understandable. However, we cannot escape the inevitable consequences of controlling behavior.

As we examine the history of the world, the negative consequences of using power to control others is legendary. Historically, we see: years of power struggles erupting into the downtrodden rising up against the establishment; those in power perpetuating the dependency of the powerless; and the police actions that spring from using power to control. Can you recognize similar patterns in your family history? The unhappy consequences this system fosters are distrust and disconnection.

People have power when they have something that others need or believe they need. In other words, one person is dependent on the other. For example:

- Parents have power because their children need love, shelter, money, etc.
- Bosses have power when employees believe they need the job
- People who are esteemed have power over those who believe they need their affirmation
- The breadwinner in a family has power over those who believe they cannot earn enough for their well-being
- Teachers have power over students who need grades
- Traditional religious leaders and spiritual gurus have power over followers who believe they need salvation and think the leader can guide them to it
- People with answers have power over people who think they need those answers
- Physicians and psychotherapists have power over clients who think they can give them health
- People who withhold love or acceptance have power over those who think they need that love or acceptance

To extricate yourself from being controlled, it is important to remember that, except for children, people in power have it only because you give it to them. Only when you believe that another person has something essential for your well-being does he or she have power over you. Since those who want to maintain control have a vested interest in keeping you dependent, your breaking out of that system means learning how to nurture yourself rather than depending upon another person to meet your needs. It is important to understand, however, that the other person will be threatened by your efforts, and will very likely not be supportive of your attempts to nurture yourself.

A truly revolutionary model for using power occurs at those times when fear is not predominant, and a Power With model emerges. When differences arise (and they always will) a process of learning is engaged in which understanding is the focus, and people feel heard, understood, and cared about. It is a cooperative process that results in solutions growing out of knowledge, personal power built out of caring, and Fulfilling Connections created from the heart.

This process begins by compassionately listening to others when a difficulty arises. It applies in parenting with issues like bringing another child into the family, discipline, bedtime, or handling chores. It applies to handling differences in business when issues arise like downsizing, broken agreements, poor workmanship, customer complaints, and performance evaluations. Likewise, this concept can be applied with mates when issues surface regarding money, dishonesty, infidelity, responsibilities, and sex.

The learning that others can experience from this approach, which includes connecting to their Heart Feelings and how to handle differences in ways that create Fulfilling Connections, is primarily dependent on how you model the use of power. Your learning will be about how to keep your heart open when faced with difficult situations. The critical step in increasing your use of the Power With model comes from an intention to resolve the fears that block Heart Feelings.

The Power With model significantly increases the effectiveness of any group because it allows learning to occur in an emotionally safe environment. It is a model that can be initiated anytime you are a leader, whether at work, in a family, or in your community. The first step is to make Fulfilling Connections a priority. Subsequent steps involve: modeling Heart Learning, especially when you lose your compassion; pointing out times when alienation, rather than Heart Feeling, is occurring; and encouraging participants to learn to viscerally feel alienation as discomfort, tension, tightness, or fear, and to acknowledge and express their feelings.

Result-oriented people, concerned that talking about feelings and accomplishing goals are mutually exclusive, may be skeptical about the practicality of sharing power. There certainly are numerous examples of attempts to share power and learn from interpersonal difficulties that wound up never getting to solutions or finished products. But this limitation can be overcome by making respectful behavior as important as accomplishing tasks and goals.

Learning to have Power With takes us out of the comfort zone of the familiar and into learning new ways that can improve relationships in every area of our lives. In the beginning, using this process takes more time; but, in the long run, resolutions that maintain Fulfilling Connections rather than accomplish short-term fixes save tremendous amounts of time. Using Power With in relationships with mates, children, and at work will be demonstrated in subsequent chapters.

The fear of being open hearted is easily understood. Feeling deeply is like standing naked. We may feel things we do not want to feel. Whether we are feeling ecstasy or pain, we are vulnerable. The fear that our feelings may lead us into difficulties makes controlling them a preeminent aspect of our lives.

We are not bad or wrong for using power to control others. We are just insecure and unaware of another alternative. The good news is that with new ways of thinking, and the courage to overcome old thinking, it is possible to forge a very different life.

Heart Learning in a Relationship Sanctuary

When two or more people engage in Heart Learning, each person feels heard, respected, and nurtured. Learning about the other and themselves is wonderful, exciting, and intimate. This is often how important new relationships begin and what precipitates falling in love. Most unhappiness in relationship results from missing the Fulfilling Connections that come from Heart Learning together and sharing Heart Feelings.

Listening and learning is what people often get from a professional therapist. The reason people fall in love with their therapist is not a big mystery. It probably has much more to do with being listened to and feeling cared about than Freud's belief that it was caused by transference of unresolved childhood feelings.

With open hearts we listen for the information that is in nature, others, and, although often very quiet, in us. Listening is surprisingly difficult for most people. While another person is speaking, our minds usually race with various thoughts, including solutions for that person's problem; judgments about the thoughts, feelings, and actions of others; thoughts about what we are going to say in return; our own difficulties; and more mundane things that take us away from the context of listening altogether. As a result, the luxury of feeling listened to provides a rare and often memorable experience. Giving this quiet, focused listening to ourselves is just as difficult, as conflicting voices of judgment and advice jockey for position in our own heads.

Fulfilling Connections occur through compassionate listening. As you connect to the feelings underneath the words of another, listening with your heart allows any negative words or energy coming from that person to pass over your head. Listening with Heart Feelings, so that the feelings of another are understood, is similar to the concept of Active Listening developed by Dr. Carl Rogers. It is also what St. Francis most likely meant when he asked God to grant him "...not so much to seek to be understood, as to understand." Compassionate listening touches all parties and provides profoundly nurturing comfort.

A common misconception is that when there are problems in a relationship, all the parties concerned need to be involved in a learning process. While it is certainly true that Fulfilling Connections between people can occur only when they are involved in learning together, it only takes one person open to Heart Learning for a relationship to transform. For this to happen requires the uncommon belief that since relationships always operate as a system, we are each equally responsible for problems in a relationship.

Most of us prefer to believe that others are primarily responsible for the problems in a relationship, and if only they would change, then everything would be all right. When we believe this, we are powerless victims. It's like one person has thrown out a line with a hook on the end and another person has bitten onto it. As they struggle, the one with the hook in her mouth shouts, "You know, if you hadn't thrown out this hook we wouldn't be having this struggle!" The one who has thrown out the hook snaps back, "Oh yeah, well if you hadn't bitten onto the hook we wouldn't be in this mess!" So long as the one who has bitten blames the one who threw and tries to get him to stop throwing out hooks, and the one who has thrown blames the one who has bitten and tries to get her to stop biting onto hooks, while they both get to be self-righteous, they are stuck.

It doesn't matter who started the fracas. Each one could focus on his or her part of the problem. She assumes personal power when she opens to learning about why she keeps biting onto hooks (which are her buttons). He assumes personal power by learning about why he keeps throwing out hooks (pushing her buttons). It only takes one of them to change for their entire system to change. When he resolves his need to bait her, there is no problem. Or alternatively, if he keeps throwing out the bait and she no longer hooks herself, there will be no struggle. Acknowledging that relationship difficulties are part of a system to which we each contribute throws off the yoke of the victim.

The focus of the second teaching story is on how learning and change can occur in a relationship when only one person in the relationship opens to Heart Learning. The two people in the story, George and Marie, have been together for six months and Marie has recently moved into George's house. The issue that precipitates their difficulty is jealousy. This is a common issue that usually leads to the deterioration of open communication and trust. Although you may find George's willingness to learn about himself not to be a typical response, the possibilities that result from such openness are very real.

TEACHING STORY #2

She Did What!?!

Differences, Disconnection, and Struggle

Fresh from winning another high profile case and satisfied that his "hotshot" reputation had been earned, George settled into his favorite chair to savor his victory with a martini. As he was playing over in his mind his "brilliant" closing argument, Marie, with her usual intensity, burst through the door and began talking about the details of her day.

Shriveled by the pin that had punctured his ego balloon, George thought, "What about me?" Putting his own news on hold, he dutifully listened as she rambled on about her asshole boss and the pettiness in her office. When the subject changed to the intelligent and charming guy who had moved into the desk next to hers, his antennae went up. He noticed a knot beginning to grow in his stomach. She noticed that her ebullience was being met by a less than enthusiastic response.

A few days later, when Marie related her walk in the park with Troy during an extended lunch, and all the new things she was learning with him, George started becoming unglued. At first, while making it clear that he was not happy with her spending that kind of time with Troy, he controlled his upset.

When she objected to his objection, his response became more animated and angry. He blurted out, "You're acting like a slut."

She tried calm reason. "You know I'm not that kind of a woman. What's wrong with talking to another man?"

"That's not the issue. This is someone you're spending more time with than you do with me. If you can't understand the problem with that, then there's something really wrong with you."

Frustrated by what she saw as his unreasonable attitude, she snapped, "Look! Neither you, nor anybody else, are going to tell me what I can and can't do. I didn't give up my apartment to come live in a prison."

Their "discussion" deteriorated into a donnybrook that ended with each of them feeling attacked and misunderstood. Whereas in the past they had become used to going to sleep "spooning" each other, that evening was spent with each clutching their own side of the bed.

The next day, George began mounting a campaign. He canvassed loyal supporters for their opinions of her outrageous behavior. Each one predictably reacted with various versions of an outraged "She did what!?!" They all agreed that she was "out of bounds" and must be stopped. Armed with more ammunition, he prepared for his next encounter.

The issue became a "cause celebre." During their ensuing battles, George and Marie took turns blaming each other for their difficulty. One time Marie self-righteously yelled, "If you didn't attack me, we wouldn't be in this fight!" Of course, she was right.

George countered with "Well, look who's talking. You've been throwing out some pretty rotten stuff! You really know how to hit below the belt." Of course, he was right.

George had thrown the first punch, and in response to his attack, she had counterpunched, and so on. Their "discussions" always ended in their now familiar back-to-back sleeping position. Their relationship descended into periods of quiet distance or angry fighting. Marie stopped volunteering anything about Troy. And when George questioned her, she answered with monosyllabic clipped sentences.

With his suspicions fueled by Marie's withheld silence, George started searching for evidence. This included snooping in her purse and eavesdropping. Finally, he found success! Tucked away in her purse he discovered a card from Troy expressing what a great time he had with her at the office party and how much he was looking forward to spending more time with her.

At dinner that night, George asked slyly, "Have you seen Troy lately?"

She responded with derisive exasperation, "George, we work together. I see him every day."

"I know that. I meant have you seen him outside of work?" George's question was not accompanied with compassion or an intent to learn. It was asked with an intent to trap. No matter how she answered, he had prepared an attack.

She, of course, fell into the trap. "No, I haven't!"

Puffed with self-righteousness he said, "You liar. I know you were at an office party with him."

Caught, Marie simultaneously felt chagrined and violated. "You son of a bitch, you've been snooping in my purse! Listen, Sherlock—or is it Shylock?—Troy and I spent some time together at the party but there's nothing going on between us." She thought to herself, "Not yet anyway, asshole."

"Well, I don't know what to believe anymore." George was feeling desperate. Fumbling in his attempts to get her to behave, he said, "If I find out there's more going on than you're telling me, both of you had better watch out! I don't know how much more of this I can take! Maybe we should just forget this relationship; I'm certainly not getting much out of it!"

George's reaction, although typical and understandable, was nevertheless unloving. Marie's reaction, although typical and understandable, was equally unloving. The wounding that resulted from their protective responses led to a predictable diminution of love, passion, and trust. Their relationship vacillated between tense periods of truces and soap opera battles.

As their relationship continued its accelerating descent into the fiery pit of unfulfilled hopes and broken dreams, George came to his wits' end. Marie was coming home later and later. Wanting to avoid the loneliness he felt whether she was there or not, he began spending more and more time at work and at a neighborhood bar.

One night, while staring into his beer, he responded to a tap on his shoulder and came face-to-face with an old friend. Putting on a happier face, he said, "Hey, Lar, it's been an age. How ya doing, and how's Allie?"

"Allie and I broke up a while ago. It was pretty rough for a while, but I'm doing better."

"Sorry to hear that." Sinking back into his previous beer face, he said, "I know what you've been going through. Marie and I are on the skids."

"Well, I'm really sorry to hear that. The two of you always seemed so happy and perfect for each other. What's been going on?"

George's now well-practiced version of events got a different response than he expected. Larry said, "You know, Georgie boy, a year ago I would have responded by telling you my story and we would have ended up blaming those bitches and getting drunk together. But I've been going through some very interesting changes lately and I'm not real interested in stories. Do you want to take a different kind of a trip?"

"What do you mean?"

"Well, from what I've been learning, all I can tell you is that if I had known then what I know now, Allie and I may have had a chance."

"Well, I'm all ears."

They found a secluded table and for the next three hours George became rapt in hearing a very different approach to life and relationships. Larry suggested some resources for George to try, and they agreed to meet again the following week.

Prior to the chance meeting with Larry, George had little interest in learning about relationships. Anytime Marie had wanted to take a personal growth workshop or share things she was learning about relationships, he had been indifferent. Now things had shifted dramatically and by the time his next meeting with Larry came along, George had prepared a whole list of questions and ideas to share.

Heart Learning

In the friendship with Larry, George embarked on a new direction of trying to win the battle of not letting his love get strangled by his fear. He confronted the parts of himself that had been malnourished. With a dedication to learning how to better nurture Marie and himself, he pulled out of feeling like a helpless victim and took "the road less traveled." Larry suggested books and movies that illustrated a different way of seeing life. George deepened his learning by meticulously keeping a journal that reflected the learning the books and movies touched off. He entitled his journal "Learning About Love." The following are some of his entries.

April 25—My talks with Larry are opening up whole new ways of seeing things, and it's not easy. Larry had to work real hard on me before I finally admitted that if anyone other than Marie had found a new and exciting friend, I would have responded with caring and joy. Responding that way seemed unrealistic, if not impossible. But I finally saw that the only things that make it difficult are the fears and beliefs that fuel my jealousy.

Larry said that compassion is the only response that preserves and deepens love, and that compassion is not conditional. He also said that the path to becoming more loving always requires confronting the demons that block its expression. In applying this to my situation with Marie, I realized that when Marie first said she had met a new person at work, I felt awful. I now know that I would have nurtured her by being happy and supportive of her developing that relationship. But I couldn't do that as long as I was so afraid of losing her. That fear caused my jealousy.

When those fears come up I need to acknowledge them and be kind to the frightened part of me, to that scared part of me where the beliefs that create my fear reside. The fear and pain need to be expressed. It's up to me to make it safe enough for that to happen.

I've realized from our talks that, no matter what the situation, when I lose my compassion and joy, fear has overcome my loving feelings for both Marie and myself. I now know that when old and deep fears are touched, I need comforting arms wrapped around me while I express my fearful feelings and come to understand and accept them. I need to be able to give that kind of nurturing to myself. This stuff is really hard.

May 2—Larry suggested that I might get a lot out of watching *The Fisher King* and so tonight I rented the video. I saw it many years ago and remember being underwhelmed, but this time I was blown away. The Robin Williams character showed me some really important things about friendship and being loving and playful. I loved the scene in the Chinese restaurant when his girlfriend is being a klutz, and rather than making fun of her, he just gets with her. I certainly haven't been that way with Marie.

Larry says that Robin Williams plays the same kind of loving and accepting person in many of his films. He particularly mentioned his roles as the psychologist in *Good Will Hunting*, the doctor in *Patch Adams*, and the teacher in *Dead Poets Society*. I'm going to watch them all.

Back to *The Fisher King*. I really identified with what a self-centered asshole the Jeff Bridges character was. His transformation into a loving person was inspiring. I know there's a lot more I can learn from that film. I wonder if Marie would like it? I think I'll watch it again tomorrow night and ask her if she's interested in joining me.

The film touched off lots of thoughts about what's really important in my life. I know there's some major learning here for me about living a simpler life. That's what the song "How About You?" is all about. It kept being repeated during the film, and now I can't get it out of my head. After the movie I wrote down the lyrics so I'm going to copy them here:

"I like New York in June, how about you?

I like a Gershwin tune, how about you?

I love a fireside when a storm is due. I like potato chips, moon light, and motor trips, how about you?

I'm mad about good books, can't get my fill.

And Franklin Roosevelt's looks give me a thrill.

Holding hands in a movie show, when all the lights are low may not be new.

But I like it, how about you?"

Catchy little tune, great words.

Maybe I'll find some answers in *Voluntary Simplicity*. When Larry suggested *The Fisher King* he also gave me that book. I guess I'll read for a while. I wonder what it has in store for me?

May 10—In one of our first talks, Larry suggested that I think about the roots of my jealousy. I'm starting to see how afraid I am of being taken advantage of, losing face with my friends, and losing Marie. I've thought that maybe I don't feel lovable or good enough, or intellectual or successful enough. One thought that really scared me was that I might not be a good enough lover.

I've had a hard time admitting to any of these beliefs. They're painful and I feel vulnerable when they come up. I've not even been consciously aware of most of them. But I'm beginning to see how they're responsible for my not being able to feel compassion for myself and for my feelings of betrayal and justifiable anger.

May 15—My fears do not justify my behavior. I need to be able to feel bad about my behavior without feeling guilty about it. That feels like a tall order. I'm not even sure I understand it yet. Given my fears and beliefs, my behavior is understandable. But that doesn't mean I have a right to do things that are disrespectful to Marie.

May 28—I have tended to hang out with people and listen only to information that supports what I want to believe. Like when I listened to the feelings and advice my buddies gave me about Marie. I never talked to people who might have given me a different perspective, like suggesting that perhaps Marie was not wrong, and that there was something important here that I could learn about myself.

Come to think of it, there were some people who hinted at other ways to see the situation. I just dismissed them and went on looking for those who believed that Marie was wrong and I was justified in doing whatever I needed to do to get her back in line.

As I see myself changing, thoughts have begun crossing my mind like "Am I going to lose my friends?" and "Are they really my friends?" This is really upsetting me. Usually, when I have upsetting thoughts, writing them down puts my mind at ease and I can go to sleep. It's not working that way this time. This must be really important. Maybe I'll just read for a while.

June 15—As I open to my fears, I'm confronting my dependency on Marie for my sense of well-being. That's why I'm so terrified of losing her. Without that fear, although I would feel terrible if she left me, it would not be the catastrophe I dread. I love Marie, but my dependency is creating the love/hate feelings that I'm realizing must accompany any dependency.

It must be no different for the compulsive eater who has a love/hate relationship with food, or the alcoholic's love/hate relationship with alcohol. Dependency puts me in the position of a child. That feels awful and certainly not powerful and affirming. When I know that I can create my own sense of well-being, I know I will be able to love Marie much more fully, in a way that leaves her feeling loved.

July 2—It's 2:00 a.m. and there's so much going on in my head that I haven't been able to sleep. Tonight I went to Larry's house to see *Eyes Wide Shut*. He had already seen it and wanted to share it with me. What an amazing film. It launched a great talk about sex and jealousy. Larry had said that the film was about how, when our vision is clouded by sex and money, we become willing to put the lives of others, and ourselves, in jeopardy. Man, did that hit home. I thought I knew a lot about sex. The more I read, the more I realize how little I know, and how much there is that Marie and I haven't talked about. I remember not wanting to see the movie when it first came out. It was the kind of film that I was afraid was too deep for me, and I was threatened by what might be stirred up. Of course, I was never that honest with myself. I think that at the time my excuse was that I was turned off by all the hype.

Anyway, it's probably a good thing I didn't see it back then. I don't think I was ready. Tonight was the perfect time. I was right though; this kind of film sure does stir things up.

August 15—I've been reading a lot about power struggles and systems that exist in relationships. The more I learn, the more I understand the death grip of the power struggle Marie and I have been in. I can see why, in a battle, there are no innocent victims. Nurturing myself means taking responsibility for my part in the mess. I can look at the hooks I throw out when I yell and try to make Marie wrong. She could look at why she bites onto those hooks. However, whether or not she chooses to do that is not my business. I just need to stay focused on my issues and by taking personal responsibility; I will nurture both of us.

Understanding that our system is like a no-fault insurance policy and acknowledging that the difficulties that result from it are created equally is paying dividends. By seeing that when Marie's fears are touched she loses compassion and that I am not totally to blame, I feel less guilty and I don't respond defensively. It also helps to remember that I can only do something about my part of the system. I won't even talk to her about her part unless—and until—she asks me. I know what I must confront to change our system. The ball is always in my court.

September 4—Tonight I saw the movie *Bliss* and I'm stunned. To see the main character learn to just hold his wife, or be sensual with her, without any demand for sex had a tremendous impact. He was even willing to move out of their home to facilitate her healing. It was the most beautiful demonstration of unconditional love I have ever seen. Hell, at one point, I couldn't even tolerate Marie going out to lunch with another guy. I know I've come a long way since then, but there's so much more to learn.

I also know I don't have to be as evolved as the guy was in the film, but it sure opened up a lot. I can't wait to call Larry tomorrow. It's so good to have someone to talk with about things like this. I really want to share some of these things with Marie—if she's interested.

September 27—When both of us get stuck in our disconnected feelings, compassion and intimate connections are impossible.

Typically, when she gets angry, I either try talking logically to her or I get angry and we wind up ranting at each other. Talking logically or arguing are both exercises in futility and frustration.

When she is experiencing disconnected feelings, she will never feel cared about by my logically trying to show her why she shouldn't feel that way. But if I were connected to my loving feelings, I wouldn't try to talk her into, or out of, anything. While she is in that state, although we can't connect intimately, I can be nurturing to myself and to her. Have I said this was hard?

October 14—I'm slowly beginning to give up my attempts to have power over Marie. I go through periods when that feels okay and, at other times, it scares the shit out of me. Control has been my middle name. How would our life and relationship look if each of us had more freedom? I guess I'll have to wait until the next chapter in my life to find out more about that one.

Being Your Own Hero, Fulfilling Connections and Possibilities

Had George been better able to allow his compassion to predominate over his fear, the following two scenarios illustrate what could have occurred at the time of Marie's bombshell.

Scenario One—This scene could take place had the initial incident occurred when George had gained some knowledge about loving relationships but had still not explored himself in great depth. It begins when Marie announces her extended lunch with Troy.

As he became aware of the knot in his stomach, he knew that his heart was not open and rather than unload on Marie he took some deep breaths and exclaimed, "God damn it, I feel like I'm going to explode!"

"Why are you so uptight? We just had an innocent lunch and we were just enjoying our friendship."

"Look, I know my jealousy is my problem, but right now it just feels like shit."

Marie felt his discomfort. "Come on. Let's sit on the couch."

He squirmed and stared at the floor for a while before he sheepishly said, "I wish I could be happy for you, but it feels like there's a cloud about to burst and I need to get you to stop this relationship."

"What are you afraid would happen if you stopped trying to control me and I was free to do whatever I want?"

With his heart open he was open to learning: "Well, for starters, maybe you'd be sexual with him."

"And then what?"

"Well, I might lose you."

Marie's head cocked and she smiled sweetly, "If I felt free to be myself and not lose your love, why in the world would I want to go anywhere else, or be with anyone else?"

George considered this for a moment. "I don't know." After another pause, "Actually, I can think of lots of reasons. He might be a better lover, or more interesting, or more fun."

"Sweetheart, I don't believe any of those things. But even if they were true, we could work those things out. The only reason I would want to leave you would be to get out from under your control."

He is struck by this simple truth that he simply had never before considered. "That makes sense but I guess I'm not sure that I really could change the things that are lacking in me."

"So you believe you're limited. I can understand that. I can think of lots of things that I think are limited about me, like my intellectual ability. It sure is a lot easier for me to see how your limited thinking is bullshit than it is to see how I limit myself."

That broke any remaining distance between them and, sinking into each other's arms, they held each other for a long time.

By responding with openness to learning, George instantly changed their system, which in the past would have had him react defensively and she get defensive in retaliation. He felt great about himself. Although she had not learned anything about her part in their old system, Marie has responded differently to George's loving behavior. She may or may not learn about her fears and unloving behavior, but in that moment, for a Fulfilling Connection to occur, it was not necessary.

Scenario Two—This scene could take place had the initial incident occurred when George's fears of inadequacy and loss were at a point where they did not become predominant when potentially difficult situations arose.

Marie burst through the door eager to tell George about the new employee who has moved into the desk next to hers. As she rambled on about how wonderful he was, and some of the new things she was learning by being with him, George looked at her lovingly.

Since he was not threatened, his heart was open and he was free to appreciate how radiant she looked when she was excited, how interesting she was when she brought new learning to him, what a wonderful energy she had, and how lucky he was to be with her. All this came out simply as "Wow, what a great time you must have had. I'm so happy for you." He felt great about himself.

With her enthusiasm freed and her happiness bubbling she could hardly stay still and she couldn't keep her hands off him. As love freed them to express the parts of themselves about which they felt best, the yarn of love entwined them. They cherished each other more than they ever imagined possible.

Another Possibility—An option available after any battle was for George and Marie to engage in a process of learning together or individually. Since they carried around many fears, which got touched off quite easily, defensive battles were to be expected. The deterioration in their relationship would not be caused by their individual battles. Their loving feelings would erode because they would not clean up their messes. This could happen after their emotions had cooled and rationality had returned, by returning to an upsetting interaction with an intention to learn from it, and to heal the wounds that had occurred from their protective responses.

It was only after many fights ending with one or both of them feeling emotionally distant that George and Marie began learning from their arguments. Even though the wounds from their disconnected encounters had gotten covered over and they were able to temporarily regain feelings of closeness, the wounds were never healed. Eventually, the scar tissue of distrust grew to the point where intimacy was a rare experience. A major part of their learning was how to heal their past hurts.

George and Marie learned that whenever they got caught in a defensive battle to separate until their emotions had subsided. Then they could learn about the fears that got them hooked and get to the place where they could be loving to each other. That learning was often done individually, after which they got back together and tried talking with one another.

Any of the loving responses illustrated in the scenarios above would have left George feeling tranquil and really good about himself. Although most relationship difficulties do not end in regaining feelings of being in love, this one was an exception. One of the primary reasons for this was George's extraordinary commitment to his personal learning and the powerful change that was possible when one person became more loving. George's change opened Marie, and changed her without her even being aware of it. As they each became renewed, so did their relationship.

The ongoing process of clearing the space between them allowed for interactions that were not possible when fear and resentment had created an environment that did not feel safe. Safety allowed for the freedom that created more and more peak experiences. George's story ends with a scene that occurred during their honeymoon. Recapturing trust and in-love feelings had allowed a clear channel of love to be present more of the time. In this particular encounter, their hearts remained open, and love infused their natural abilities for a prolonged experience of Fulfilling Connection. It was described in the following entry from his "Learning About Love" journal (George had become quite a romantic and loved writing. He worked on this description for a long time before entering it):

The warm and cloudless day called us to a hike. We rode bikes to the trailhead, locked them to a fence and began our journey. The fall colors were peaking. The reds and browns of the scrub oak mixed with evergreens to produce a palette that transfixed us. We stopped on a small wooden footbridge spanning the creek to smell and stare at nature's resplendence.

We hugged each other, expressing our gratitude for being alive, in paradise, and in love. Moving up the trail we giggled and held hands as we traversed the river, climbing over boulders, sloshing through mud, and wading in the shallow parts of the creek. Not being on a schedule allowed us the rare experience of wandering. We discovered new colors, found hidden life forms, fed the squirrels that brazenly took food out of our hands, and felt one with nature. We laughed when I expressed the realization that it was probably necessary to wander in order to find wonder.

When we reached the high meadow at the top of the creek, the entire hillside was covered with multicolored leaves. This was our backdrop as we sat down to eat lunch. Our noontime show included a family of deer who, although keeping a respectable distance, seemed to be joining us.

After some more hiking, playing, and exploring, we headed back down the trail. We started running. Losing any self-consciousness and abandoning any messages that told me to be careful, I blended with the environment and felt like the Native Americans who had once summered in these mountains. I stopped to rest and waited for Marie. We sat for a long time relating our experiences. Both of us had experienced losing fear and becoming one with the mountain. It was incredible. We continued our journey, clutching hands whenever possible.

George and Marie were creating a relationship sanctuary. Increasing trust and respect and, therefore, increasing our moments of Fulfilling Connections is rarely accomplished alone. Although human accomplishments are a testament to the creative magnificence of our minds, this most amazing instrument also has the ability to be deceptive and deceitful, not only with others but also with ourselves. For this reason, friendships in which Heart Learning is an integral part of the relationship is an invaluable part of the journey toward being your own hero.

Such friendships can be a part of any relationship. They can be outside of primary relationships or they can be with a mate, parent, employee, or boss. Developing them requires a conscious effort. It involves seeking people who place a very high value on personal learning and have developed the intellectual ability and emotional awareness to challenge you with empathy. They are the real-life angels who drop in when you are ready.

Actually, they are around all the time, but as the ancient saying goes, "When the student is ready, the teacher will appear." They are found in many places, including classes relating to personal and spiritual growth, book clubs, self-help therapy groups, and religious institutions that have an abiding orientation to empowering individuals. They are rarely found in bars, malls, sports arenas, or on television.

If such angels have not yet graced your life, perhaps the idea popularized in the film *Field of Dreams*,—"If you build it, they will come"—will help you keep the faith that it will happen.

Chapter Five

Open Hearts With Mates

*Beyond the fields of right doing and wrong doing is another field.
I'll meet you there.*

—Rumi

Being in love is one of life's most preoccupying desires. Without it, where would music, poetry, art, film, literature, and businesses that sell and advertise weight loss, cosmetics, and fashions be? And the reason is quite simple. Two hearts opening together produce the tremendous vigor, unbounded optimism, profound serenity, and passionate sexuality that result in the peak experiences that often seem like miracles.

An experience that may be nice by oneself takes on profoundly expanded dimensions when it is part of a Fulfilling Connection with a loved one. For example, having a sexual experience by oneself or with a casual partner may feel good. It may satisfy a sexual need and provide pleasure and temporary relief. But an experience in which Heart Feelings flow freely is distinctly different from merely satisfying a sexual urge. A Fulfilling Connection during a sexual experience is truly "making love." It is a delicious and profoundly satisfying adventure.

Although maintaining the dream-like ecstasy of being in love seems like a fairy tale, the commonly held idea that the erosion of these feelings is a natural part of getting to know someone is false. When Heart Feelings persist, being with another person continues to be exciting and wonderful. The diminution of Heart Feelings and Fulfilling Connections is a very identifiable step-by-step process of hearts becoming encased.

The openness that is essential for love and intimacy lasts only until something happens that feels threatening or frightening. It may occur as a thought such as "Uh oh I could really fall head-over-heels for this person." Or, it might be something the other person inadvertently says or does that upsets us. Rather than expressing our upset, we shut down ever so slightly, and a brick is put in place.

The other person senses this withdrawal, usually without even consciously knowing it and responds with a brick of his or her own. The first person senses this withdrawal, usually unconsciously, and withdraws a little more. Neither person's hurt is resolved, and a system that results in fear and distance is established. Each person will continue his or her retreat, placing one brick at a time into an ever-thickening wall. After a while, encrusted hearts make Fulfilling Connections impossible.

The next teaching story begins with a common couple conflict over money and describes the distrust and emotional deadness that inevitably follows disconnection from their hearts. By engaging in Heart Learning, the couple emerges into new possibilities.

TEACHING STORY #3

He Said/She Said

Differences, Disconnection, and Struggle

Monthly bills in hand, Bill leaned back in his swivel chair, shaking his head in exasperation. Mary had once again broken her agreement not to buy presents except for birthdays and special holidays. With a familiar irritation in his body, he silently asked himself, "What do I have to do to get through to this woman? I've been very patient, haven't I?"

In his mind he went through his ritual litany of self-serving justifications to prove that he had indeed gone beyond the call of duty. "I have painstakingly worked with her to get her to see the reality of our financial situation. I have had her sit with me while I pay the bills each month. I have helped her become familiar with the income and liabilities sheet I meticulously keep on the computer. What more can I do?" he again asked the invisible, universal source of wisdom.

Satisfied with the "Nothing" he received, he was ready to confront Mary. As he again prepared himself to get her to be more responsible, he thought, "Just be nice and don't get angry." But, without the compassion that would have naturally guided an intention to learn about either her or himself, no matter how he approached her, his intent to get Mary to change would not be heartfelt. He called out a saccharine, "Honey, we need to talk." He closed his eyes, took a deep breath and began slowly counting to ten.

In another room, Mary dutifully got up and began her journey toward the den. For many years Mary had tried to understand Bill's way of thinking. She had tried to curb her spending. She had tried to concentrate as she sat with him at the computer as he explained his intricate accounting system. Mary knew she was not a spendthrift, but she did like to buy things for the house or presents for her family and friends—things that Bill thought were unnecessary.

In the past she had tried showing Bill the logic behind her way of thinking, but these attempts usually degenerated into unpleasant scenes. Lately, although she had been really trying to "control" her spending, at times she just couldn't seem to help herself. Each time she indulged her desires she assured herself that this time, rather than thinking of the money, Bill would appreciate how considerate she was of others.

Mary never considered the fact that, given Bill's fears and beliefs, the reaction she expected would have been a miracle. Unless something happened to radically change his consciousness, his responses would stay true to form. If Bill were a character in a play, and upon receiving the monthly bills reacted as Mary expected, the audience would be stupefied. But rather than acknowledge the unreality of her expectations, Mary continued to hope and invariably wound up feeling the devastation of a martyr.

Whether it was his tone, or an airborne zing of extrasensory energy, Mary sensed Bill's irritation before she ever entered the room, and a familiar tension began radiating from her stomach into her arms and legs. She had learned that "We need to talk" never meant "We're going to have a loving exploration." It always meant she was going to hear what she had done wrong. She had experienced the same dynamic as a child whenever her parents had been upset with her. Naturally, she dreaded "talking."

In general, other than their ongoing money issue, Mary and Bill had a comfortable relationship. They had a nice home, two wonderful children, and were very civil with each other. Neither was interested in thinking deeply about things or talking about their feelings, so they rarely discovered anything new about themselves or each other, but that had never seemed to be a problem.

They had settled into a routine that did not cause either of them much upset. They talked about safe things like the weather, what the kids or neighbors were doing, and world events. When they went out, it was to see a family movie. Their second television was rarely used because they even liked the same shows.

Mary and Bill had no idea that their needs for Fulfilling Connections to themselves and each other were not being met, and that their lives were in a holding pattern. Their relationship sheltered them and they could not imagine being with anyone else or living anywhere else.

They could have continued living this way without ever realizing the cost of avoiding potentially dangerous situations. The flame of passion that sparked when they first met had long since diminished. The risk of that flame being rekindled in another relationship lay as an unseen, but very real threat.

Mary and Bill had many acquaintances, but few close friends. They had one group of friends that had been meeting together socially for the past year. Five couples gathered together on a rotating basis in one of their homes for dinner and a pleasant evening of catching up on each other's lives.

On one such occasion Mary and Bill entered their monthly meeting with an uneasy tension between them. Earlier in the day they had had one of their difficult discussions about money. In the past, Mary had been able to forget such disagreements and put on a happy face when they were with others. But this time she just couldn't seem to get the things he said out of her mind.

After dinner, Mary and Joyce were alone tidying up in the kitchen when Joyce put her arms around Mary and asked, "Are you okay?"

For the first time in her life, Mary allowed her dam to break. Through an ocean of tears, she shared her pent-up unhappiness about being treated like a child by Bill. She not only said things that she had never shared with anyone before, but some of the things that came out she had not even allowed herself to know before that evening.

The muffled sobs heard through the door made everyone else uneasy, but they pretended as if nothing out of the ordinary was going on. When the kitchen door began opening, their strained conversations immediately stopped and all heads snapped toward the door. The obvious signs that it was Mary who had been crying particularly embarrassed Bill. As soon as the obligatory and automatic "What's going on?" escaped his lips, he knew he would be sorry he asked.

Mary said quietly, "I guess there's a lot I've been holding back. Joyce and I have had a very enlightening talk."

As the women's eyebrows raised and their ears perked, the men sagged in dread. They huddled closer as Mary summarized what she and Joyce had been sharing. It sparked the liveliest discussion the group had ever had.

Three of the couples identified with problems around communication and intimacy, while the other two did not. By the end of the evening the three couples interested in these issues decided that they would meet an additional time each month to talk about their relationships.

Heart Learning

The first meeting of the new group was at the home of Joyce and Ted. After a quick potluck dinner, they gathered in the den. Joyce began the meeting. "I've been saving an article that describes a couples' group doing what we're wanting to do. In addition to regular meetings that include discussing books and movies, they also do things like creating holiday rituals, some of which include their families and some of which are spent with only group members. And, there's even a phone number to call for more information.

"One other thing," Joyce continued. "This group feels that the most important thing responsible for their success is their values statement. It's a pretty simple one, so I copied it for each of us." She passed out the following statement:

> To become more loving, we focus on compassion, respect, and learning. We seek to deepen our understanding of compassionate and respectful behavior by evaluating everything that we do through the filter of whether it facilitates a loving connection.

Everyone was excited by the idea of patterning their group on the same basic principles as the group introduced to them by Joyce. They agreed to be thinking about a values statement that would be appropriate for their group and to spend some time at their next meeting crafting their own unique statement.

At that point in the evening, there seemed to be a sense of completion and Ted suggested that perhaps they could watch the second half of a football game that he was particularly interested in.

"Hold on a minute!" Joyce exclaimed, "I've got another idea. It's still early, and on the chance that we might be done early, I rented a movie that I thought might be fun to see together and discuss."

They all agreed to watch *Pleasantville*.

As Joyce had hoped, one of the film's major devices in which the characters become colorized when they expressed undeveloped parts of themselves, provoked a lively discussion as each person talked about those undeveloped elements of their own lives. After the discussion, Bill commented, "I'd like to see that film again."

"I often do that," Joyce quickly added. "I get so much more out of a film the second time. Upon a second or third viewing, I see lots of things that I missed the first time."

Everyone was very enthusiastic about their evening, but none more than Joyce. For years, she had felt alone with her interest in relationships. Now she could "come out of the closet" and share the books and movies she had longed to discuss with others. She couldn't wait to suggest movies like *Secrets and Lies* and *Lantana* and her favorite relationship book, *Love and Awakening*, by John Welwood.

Learning about being more intimate took Mary and Bill on a road that led to the wellspring of their problems—their need for control and the loss of Heart Feelings that resulted from their controlling behaviors. They went slowly, but the more they learned, the more dedicated they became to learning about themselves and their relationship.

Occasionally they needed help from professionals, but usually they found what they needed to get over any rough spots from other group members and from books. Along the road they looked at Mary's need to please and Bill's hardness when he became judgmental.

Growing up, Mary had learned that a "good girl" never displeased anyone, and that if someone was unhappy with her, she had done something wrong. With men in particular, she had learned that the way to keep a man happy was "to make herself less to make him more." To protect herself from being wrong and suffering rejection from both her inner critic and from others, Mary had learned to limit herself by putting the needs of others ahead of her own.

Mary never "made waves." On the contrary, she received lots of kudos for her easy-going approach to life. A major reason she had never really expressed her feelings, explored her capacity for learning, or manifested her productivity, however, was that she tried very hard to keep herself safe from failure and disapproval.

When she did not get the appreciation she wanted, she either "sucked it up like a good girl" or she cried. On those rare occasions when she broke down, she felt either like a bad person deserving of approbation, or else felt that unreasonable demands were being made of her. Either way, she assumed the consciousness of a victim: "Poor me, I'm just hopeless" or "Poor me, I'm just misunderstood."

Without the self-compassion that would have allowed her not to take the upsets of others personally, she piled on huge helpings of blame. The consequences of this dynamic spilled into many areas of her life as her self-doubts and fears were kept in place and her aliveness was muted.

She realized that although she had fallen in love with someone who took care of her financially, she resented being in that position. This was evidenced by her vacillations between rebellion and compliance. She sometimes surreptitiously rebelled against the yoke Bill had given her and which she willingly kept around her neck. At other times, she went along with "the program" but resented Bill. Either way, she felt bad about herself and their relationship suffered from the strains of resentment and fear.

When upsets did occur, Mary did not engage in in-depth discussions because of her fears that such interactions might deteriorate into one of them feeling bad. Her attempts to placate Bill did not nurture her because denying how she really felt compromised her integrity. They did not nurture Bill because they shielded him from the opportunity to confront many things he did that created disconnection—for example, his need for control and how his controlling behavior affected others, and his beliefs and fears about money.

Bill thought of himself as an easy-going, generous, and loving person. He occasionally felt irritated, but only for what he believed were "justifiable reasons." Like most people, he had a sacrosanct list of clearly egregious behaviors that justified unloving behavior. Broken agreements were at the top of his list.

In learning about himself, Bill confronted questions like: Why did I marry a woman who does not earn her own money and is thus dependent on me? If I so dislike being responsible for our finances, why did I marry a woman who I knew had a proclivity toward spending and was not interested in a career? Even though being in control is a great burden, what do I gain from it? Do I need to keep a tight rein on her as a way of keeping myself under control?

Although allowing himself to feel the fears underneath his irritation left Bill feeling vulnerable, it opened him to new and important learning about how to be more loving toward himself and Mary. Understanding and connecting with his compassion helped him become more self-accepting.

With compassion, he began seeing the deep discomfort and sadness in the person at the other end of his diatribes. He also saw the effect his self-righteous behavior had on others. For example, how his failure to offer the support that might have aided Mary in overcoming her disconnection from her Heart Feelings and subsequent lack of personal power helped perpetuate that disconnection.

He explored the possibility that Mary becoming more personally powerful was threatening to him. The self-doubts that kept him from rejoicing in the emergence of a more secure Mary were kept in place by his behavior. Those lurking self-doubts kept him from being more open and loving—the behavior that would have left him feeling better about himself.

Their fears and beliefs had left them both wounded. The knee-jerk defensive responses that allowed them to avoid dealing with their fears had created a well-entrenched system. As they engaged in a continuing learning process, they and their system slowly began changing.

There were breakthroughs and backslides. During their learning process they tenderly saw themselves and each other more honestly while experiencing more moments of Fulfilling Connection. As they nurtured one another they became more important to each other and their love grew.

Being Your Own Hero, Fulfilling Connections and Possibilities

With the learning and understanding Bill and Mary were gaining, the way they responded to differences would have looked entirely different from the time this story began. For example, with monthly bills in hand and compassion in his heart, Bill would have approached Mary with genuine curiosity and gently might have said, "Sweetheart, I notice that you've spent more than what we agreed upon. I'd really like to understand what's going on, and especially what my part of this difficulty might be." In this safe environment Mary would have been much more likely to explore her own issues.

But, even had Bill approached her with irritation, if Mary's compassion was predominant, she would have seen the pain under his irritation and responded with loving understanding, "Gee, honey, I can see this is really upsetting you. Do you want to talk about it?"

In either of the above scenarios, a compassionate response would have left both of them feeling really good about themselves and at the same time opened the door to uncovering many new questions and possibilities. Finding answers, however, would not have been paramount. More important would have been the process of discovery in which they were involved.

By opening to learning about themselves, seeing each other's insecurities, and creating a safe space to explore themselves, they would have created Fulfilling Connections and thus nurtured their Heart Feelings. They literally and figuratively would have put their arms around each other while encouraging each other's journey toward confronting their demons.

While exploring their disconnected feelings and how to retain their Heart Feelings, they would occasionally have had some rough interactions. Their fears would always be with them, but the power of their fears would diminish. As they gained the strength that would allow their compassion to predominate more of the time, their interactions would be significantly different and their moments of Fulfilling Connections would increase.

One such occasion occurred not long after they had begun their Heart Learning process. While engaged in a sexual experience, Bill lost his erection. Obviously disturbed, he rolled over and stared silently at the ceiling.

Mary turned toward him. Propping herself on her elbow, she ran her other hand caressingly through his thinning salt and pepper hair and said, "Do you want to talk?"

"No!" he replied curtly.

"Okay, but just remember that I love you, and when you're ready I would love to explore what's going on."

She lay back and considered what she wanted to do until Bill was available. She decided to read for a while. Switching on her nightstand light, she picked up a book, stuffed two pillows behind her head, and plunged into her novel.

After a few minutes, she reached out to let him know that she was available by placing her hand on his arm. He didn't respond and when her arm became uncomfortable she withdrew it.

Another few minutes passed. Finally, Bill turned toward her and put his hand on her stomach. She reached down and cupped her hand over his. He propped himself up on his elbow and said, "I want to talk, but I'm scared."

Putting down her book and looking softly into his eyes she said, "What's going on?"

"I'm scared that what I have to say may upset you and I don't want to hurt you."

"I appreciate your concern, sweetheart, but you know that I'm learning to take better care of myself and I'm not so fragile. I can deal with my hurt. Is there anything else that you might be concerned about?"

He took a few deep breaths. He was having trouble looking her in the eyes. "I guess I'm also scared of how you're going to react. I know it's been a long time since you've withdrawn, but I'm still afraid that you might shut down."

She smiled lovingly. "Well, I guess we each still have our tender areas, but I'm ready to get into whatever comes up when you are."

He took some even deeper breaths. "A long time ago when we weren't as close as we are now, I stopped feeling very turned on by you. I got into the habit of using fantasy to maintain my erection, but tonight I couldn't."

Mary was devastated. She wanted to scream at him for keeping her down all those years and then now telling her that she wasn't attractive enough for him. She wanted to blame herself for being such a wimp. She wanted to blame this crazy-making culture for giving her the messages about her body and her sexuality that filled her with so much fear. All this and more she wanted to spew all over him.

Although compassion was not her primary emotion at the moment, she tried to put what she had been learning into practice. "That really hurts and I am pissed. I know there's pain underneath my anger, but right now I feel like I just want to beat the shit out of you."

Bill felt compassion and thought he could maintain a loving space while she vented her anger. "I knew you would be upset and I'm ready to hear your anger, so have at me."

From the abyss of her anger, Mary blasted him. As it spilled out all over him, rather than taking it personally and thinking about what he was going to say in defense, he just listened and felt her deep pain. As she started winding down, his tears started building.

With her magazine of anger spent and lying harmlessly between them, her sadness bubbled forth. When she looked at Bill and saw his caring and vulnerability, her dam burst. They collapsed into a very moist embrace.

As they each felt the pain from the past, they silently held each other for a long time. So much had been stirred up that it was hard to talk. When they finally broke their silence, he held her while she cried over her missed opportunities to develop her many unique talents and abilities. Then, she held him as he felt and explored the pain of contributing to her self-doubts with his criticism.

Their exploration lasted for hours. At 1:00 a.m., as they lay exhausted in each other's arms, Bill became aware of how good it felt to have his limp penis touching her leg, and he noticed that his tiredness was lifting. When he moved his hand to gently touch her breast, his penis began feeling even better and more alive.

As they caressed each other with their mouths and tongues, Mary noticed her own sexual feelings beginning to stir. Her hand reached for his penis. They looked at each other and playfully smiled. Bill said, "Wait a minute, I'll be right back." He quickly put a CD in the stereo, pushed the play button, and hurried back to bed. As their favorite romantic music filled everything and every body in the room, they resumed their horizontal dance.

Being fully present and turned-on to her produced new feelings in him. Looking into her eyes he experienced her magnificence. True, she had always been beautiful to him, but this time he saw beyond the physical into the special place where the unadulterated soft and innocent person resided.

The music informed his hands and, depending on where the notes directed them, they circled or stroked, lingered or roamed, played or caressed. He entered her easily and gently with a shudder that coursed through his entire body. The mixture of passion and serenity felt like coming home. They didn't move. They just looked at each other, allowing the delicious feelings of ecstasy to fill every part of their bodies.

They shared their deep connection for a long time as the music from *Les Miserables* played in the background. When Jean Valjean sang, "To love another person is to see the face of God," pent-up tears began to take their leave. As sobs convulsed his entire body, Bill became immobilized and collapsed onto her. Grateful for the opportunity to share these wonderful moments, they just held each other tightly.

As he experienced love in a deeper way than he had ever known, he noticed a pang of fear. He decided to let it go, but made a mental note to explore that fear with Mary at another time. For now, he just wanted to immerse himself in her beauty and their love.

Although their subsequent explorations did not always end in a sexual experience, their talking very often was lovemaking. At those times, each of them felt completely satisfied as they fell asleep in each other's arms, filled with appreciation for having each other on this journey.

Heart Learning as a Couple

Having the objectivity and courage to take responsibility for our part of any situation with which we are unhappy, and wanting to learn more about the nature of that unhappiness, is an indispensable part of Heart Learning. Most people fight this idea tooth and nail. To paraphrase a line sung by Professor Henry Higgins in *My Fair Lady*, "I'd prefer a new edition of the Spanish Inquisition, than to ever see my part in all this strife."

In twenty years as a marriage counselor, I never encountered one person entering therapy for a relationship difficulty who had an intention to learn about his or her part of the difficulty. On the contrary, each partner was convinced that if only the other person changed, he or she would be happy. Each had cultivated a finely honed litany of complaints identifying the other person's shortcomings. Self-righteously they would proclaim "We're not intimate because he doesn't share his feelings" or "We're not closer because she's too demanding" and so on. They often brought in books with the corners turned down on pages that contained brightly highlighted statements of experts who supported their position.

Heart Learning requires taking your eyes off others, thus ceasing being a victim and playing the blame game and taking responsibility for your part in the problem, thus becoming more personally powerful. This will hold true as we explore difficulties in parenting and at work in the chapters that follow.

In a Heart Learning process, each person feels heard, respected, and nurtured. Learning about another and oneself is wonderful, exciting, and intimate. This is often how important new relationships begin and it is this learning that precipitates falling in love. Most unhappiness in relationships results from missing the Fulfilling Connections that come from sharing Heart Learning and Heart Feelings.

Imagine what might result from such openness and caring with your partner. Imagine your partner feeling safe enough to open to his or her personal learning and the excitement, satisfaction, and intimacy of learning important things together. That kind of tender, loving, and nurturing interaction facilitates important growth in each person and ends in a highly enjoyable and meaningful evening.

A common concern of many people is "What if the other person is not open to learning about himself or herself?" That certainly is a possibility. All you can do is open the door for learning. In a disconnected interaction, that door is blocked. When your own Heart Feelings are present, there is a greater possibility that the other person will walk through the door that you have opened. Although they may miss a golden opportunity by not taking advantage of the open door, you have still made it a little safer for him or her to walk through it at a later time.

It is also possible that another person may never be interested in self-knowledge. You cannot have control over another person's choices—all you can do is perhaps influence those choices by your own openness. When another person does not open to you or to himself or herself, you cannot be intimate with him or her—but you will have achieved something very valuable: the self-esteem that accompanies staying connected to your Heart Feelings. Hopefully, it is becoming clearer that giving up control and thereby allowing your Heart Feelings to be more in evidence is what makes this process so beautiful and so rare.

The bricks that encase our hearts result from differences that are reacted to in unloving ways. Responses may range from trying to use power to withdrawing into indifference, but they all result from a disconnection to one's heart. The issues that precipitate this disconnection are endless and, at the bottom line, not even that important. Issues might involve sex, money, religion, time, other relationships, or work; but it really does not matter what the issue is. How the issue is responded to is what creates Fulfilling Connections or disconnection.

When we are in love, differences over an issue tap into many fears that surround another person having power and authority, such as being controlled, helpless, lonely, inadequate, abandoned, and foolish. Many of these fears have a primal connection to our family of origin. For example, men often fear a woman having the power their mother did when they needed both their mother's love and to establish their own identity. As a child, a man's responses may have included actively rebelling against his mother's control, accommodating to her demands but resisting passively, accommodating to her demands and giving up his individuality, or any combination of the above.

Being in love places a man back on the horns of his childhood dilemma. When differences arise, his responses will most likely mirror the deeply engrained patterns he established in childhood. Until he resolves his power and authority issues he is stuck. The feelings and responses that once were his lifeline now serve to frustrate his need for Fulfilling Connections.

Exploration of issues always winds down into looking at our desire for power and control as a way to protect ourselves from our fear of losing control. In a Heart Learning process, over time, either the issue changes or our response changes. Either way, Fulfilling Connections grow.

The "Paths Through Conflict" chart for couples that follows first appeared in *Do I Have to Give Up Me to Be Loved by You?* which Margaret and I co-authored almost twenty years ago and was only slightly amended for the revised edition of the book published in March 2002. To a great extent, the continuing popularity of the book lies in the simplicity of the ideas conceptualized in that chart. Looking at relationship conflicts through the lens of that chart provides a very useful template for understanding the difference between the openhearted responses that lead to Fulfilling Connections (the right side of the chart) and responses that come from a disconnection to one's heart and lead to dissatisfaction (the left side of the chart). Variations of that chart applying the same basic ideas to parenting and work-related conflicts appear in subsequent chapters.

THE PATHS THROUGH CONFLICT

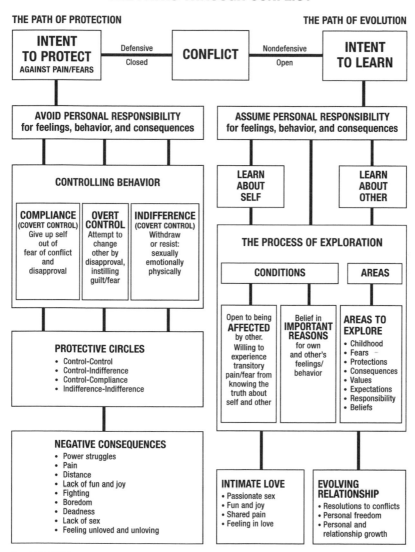

Applying the Paths Through Conflict Chart

To illustrate using the chart, a most common relationship issue will be used as an example: You expected your loved one home hours ago.

At 10:00 p.m. you call the place where he or she had been and there is no answer. You become more and more concerned. You call other places without luck. By 11:30 p.m., you have reached your breaking point and are ready to call the Highway Patrol, hospitals, etc. This is not the first time he or she has been late, but the lateness has never been so egregious.

Finally, you hear the familiar sound of his or her car pull into the driveway and you peak through the curtain. You breathe a sigh of relief and begin moving toward the door. In the brief moments between window and door, anger starts to build. When the door opens you explode, "Where the hell have you been? I've been worried sick. What happened, did you break your dialing finger?! Why are you so inconsiderate?! You're so selfish. If you really cared about me you wouldn't treat me this way."

Your tirade is met with a litany of defensive excuses and reasons why you should not feel the way you do: "I knew this was going to happen. If I had called you and told you where I was, you would have been upset. What's the big deal if I'm a little late? You're always so uptight. I feel as if I'm suffocating in this relationship."

Finally, in exasperation you break down in tears and say, "Don't you know how much I care about you? I wouldn't be so upset if I didn't love you as much as I do."

Things get patched up but neither of you feels heard, or cared about. The wounds are raw and there is a palpable distance between you.

In this situation, you became protected (left side of the chart) and your compassion got lost. The other person felt only the coldness of your anger, self-righteousness, and irritation. These feelings were communicated through a veil of hardness that ranged from clipped tones to hysterical anger. The other person felt attacked and did not experience concern and sadness for you because he or she had become disconnected from his or her compassion.

Disconnection from your heart:

- Protected you from your more vulnerable feelings of concern and sadness

- Produced disconnecting behavior—for example, yelling and lectures
- Resulted in an alienating defensive battle

The person on the other end of your tirade could have been either a teenage child or an adult. In the face of an attack, most people react by either closing up and shrinking away in guilt or by fighting back.

Your Heart Feelings were buried under your desire to try and get him or her to behave differently to protect yourself from going through those awful feelings—again. With fear dominant, your intent was to try to get him or her to feel sorry for you, to feel guilty for having caused you so much pain, and to fear the wrath of your disapproval. Your expectation was that by instilling these feelings you could control his or her behavior and he or she would no longer be late. None of this truly nurtured the other person or you. None of this conveyed your caring.

Knowing what you would have felt and how you would have responded if fear and Disconnecting Beliefs were not there (right side of the chart) is sometimes difficult. To fully understand this you have to imagine what the response would be of a good friend who was not feeling threatened by the situation.

An open heart spawns the behavior that lets others know you care and produces soft and warm inquiries like "Are you okay?" If another person's lateness was caused by unavoidable circumstances, such as an accident, comforting him or her and your relief in knowing that he or she is well follows naturally.

If the lateness was not caused by a physical infirmity, compassion might move you to want to know about personal issues relating to his or her lateness. With a sincere intent to understand, your responses might include inquires like "What's going on?" and "Why does this keep happening?" Underlying this heartfelt desire to understand would be the belief that the other person had very good reasons for his or her behavior, so you might ask, "Is there something I'm doing that you're reacting to?" This is a far cry from the nonnurturing responses of coldly judging the other person as wrong, bad, and inconsiderate.

An intent to learn about yourself would take you into all the issues that have already been discussed in this book related to the fears and Disconnecting Beliefs that blocked your Heart Feelings.

As you consider the description of Heart Feelings and Heart Learning in this chapter, ask yourself, "How does such openness feel?" Is it hard to imagine or does it seem unrealistic? Does it feel too vulnerable? Is there a fear that the other person might take advantage of you, not care about you, be hard and defensive and/or use your softness against you? (As you read the previous sentence, if your mind wanted to substitute "weakness" for "softness" you have an important direction for your learning.) Your answers to the above questions are pointing toward the beliefs that keep your Heart Feelings at bay.

It is usually much easier to see why attacking or withdrawing—the two sides of the disconnection coin—are not nurturing towards others than it is to see why disconnected feelings and behaviors are not nurturing for yourself. The simple reason is that when you are disconnected from compassion, your heart is closed: You feel tense, your self-esteem is eroded, and your aloneness is perpetuated.

To experience this, contrast the feelings in your body when you are angry and how you feel when you are caring, soft, and open. Which do you like best? Which makes you feel proud of who you are and personally powerful? Which creates a warm connection with another? Which communicates your love and acceptance? Which allows the space for an exciting and satisfying learning process? Which do you want?

This process is not for those who insist that it feels better to be angry, self-righteous, and distant. It is for those who realize that immediate defensive, disconnecting responses do not bring the Fulfilling Connections they want and are motivated to immerse themselves in a process leading to ameliorating that behavior.

Compassion nurtures you because it allows you to see how loving you are. Heart Learning nurtures you because it opens the door for learning important things regarding the fears and Disconnecting Beliefs that create your protections and the path toward healing those wounds. In the dialogue that might follow, you could uncover some of the very important reasons that contributed to creating an unsafe environment, such as your fear of the future, lack of faith in it, difficulty in creating your happiness when another is not emotionally present, and your need for control.

This is only a small sample of what there is to learn from upsets. As Heart Learning deepens and the number of Fulfilling Connections increase, you will learn the important lessons contained within upsets and may even come to appreciate them.

Intimacy

In a relationship sanctuary, intimacy flourishes. With an open heart, we are intimate with ourselves, and when hearts open together, we are intimate with others.

I believe the book that best describes the meaning and challenge of intimacy is *The Invitation* by Oriah Mountain Dreamer (Harper San Francisco, 1999). As you read the poem that is the basis of the book, try staying aware of both the longing and the fear that it evokes.

The Invitation

It doesn't interest me what you do for a living. I want to know what you ache for, and if you dare to dream of meeting your heart's longing.

It doesn't interest me how old you are. I want to know if you will risk looking like a fool for love, for your dream, for the adventure of being alive.

It doesn't interest me what planets are squaring your moon. I want to know if you have touched the center of your own sorrow, if you have been opened by life's betrayals or have become shriveled and closed from fear of further pain. I want to know if you can sit with pain, mine or your own, without moving to hide it or fade it or fix it.

I want to know if you can be with joy, mine or your own, if you can dance with wildness and let the ecstasy fill you to the tips of your fingers and toes without cautioning us to be careful, to be realistic, to remember the limitations of being human.

It doesn't interest me if the story you are telling me is true. I want to know if you can disappoint another to be true to yourself; if you can bare the accusation of betrayal and not betray your own soul; if you can be faithless and therefore trustworthy.

I want to know if you can see beauty, even when it is not pretty every day, and if you can source your own life from its presence.

I want to know if you can live with failure, yours and mine, and still stand on the edge of the lake and shout to the silver of the full moon, "Yes!"

It doesn't interest me to know where you live or how much money you have. I want to know if you can get up, after the night of grief and despair, weary and bruised to the bone, and do what needs to be done to feed the children.

It doesn't interest me who you know or how you came to be here. I want to know if you will stand in the center of the fire with me and not shrink back.

It doesn't interest me where or what or with whom you have studied. I want to know what sustains you, from the inside, when all else falls away.

I want to know if you can be alone with yourself and if you truly like the company you keep in the empty moments.

Although most people have experienced intimacy, it is typically a fleeting and infrequent occurrence. Increasing moments of intimacy are achieved by only a select number of people, not because they possess skills that the rest of do not, but because they put a high premium on staying connected to their hearts. The time and effort that George and Marie, and Bill and Mary, the two couples in Teaching Stories #2 and #3, put into themselves and their relationships paid off in delicious experiences of intimacy. But, for continuing and deepening moments of intimacy, Heart Learning is necessary during the course of an entire lifetime.

At times in this process, you may get discouraged and ask yourself, "Is it worth it?" A better question is "What choice do I have?" During difficult times, it's important to remember that if you want a life of adventure with serenity, rather than excitement and passion being found through the melodrama of constant crisis, there is no alternative.

Chapter Six

Open Hearts With Children

Then it was as if I suddenly saw the secret beauty of their hearts, the depths where neither sin nor desire can reach, the person that each one is in God's eyes. If only they could see themselves as they really are. If only we could see each other that way there would be no reason for war, for hatred, for cruelty . . . I suppose the big problem would be that we would all fall down and worship each other.

—Thomas Merton

The desire to have children is as fundamental as the desire for love with another adult. Being with a newborn is one of life's most joyous and memorable events. It's like falling in love all over again. For many of the same reasons that erode in-love feelings with our mates, those feelings with our children typically become frozen moments in time "Kodak moments" that no longer represent the truth of the present reality. The good news is that with expanded Heart Feelings, renewed Fulfilling Connections with our children can become more a part of our everyday lives.

Our entire approach to parenting shifts when learning to be a more loving person becomes an important reason for having children. Unfortunately, most ideas about parenting do not address the idea of keeping our hearts open when faced with difficulties. Traditional wisdom usually imparts only ideas for better controlling children. Even books that present nontraditional child-raising ideas usually offer little help in keeping our hearts open in the trenches of everyday life.

Of the four books that I coauthored with Dr. Margaret Paul, the one I have always thought is the most important is *Do I Have to Give Up Me to Be Loved By My Kids* (originally titled, *If You Really Loved Me*). Yet, this book did not sell well and the few remaining copies are available only from the authors. The question of why has haunted me for years.

One possibility is that focusing on asking parents to learn more about what it means to be loving in upsetting situations with their children is not what most people want. Parents are often looking for quick-fix techniques to get their children to behave. If you have read this far, this likely is not true of you or you would have long ago given up on the concepts put forth here. The focus of this chapter is to look at what it means to let go of trying to change our children and what can happen when we learn to keep our hearts open more of the time.

Before Margie and I had children, we talked long and seriously about how we wanted to raise them. Although very dedicated and loving parents had raised us, we wanted to do better. I think we did pretty well with child raising, yet we, just like our parents, were operating within our own psychological limitations.

For example, nothing prepared us to deal with a fiercely independent one-year-old. I am convinced that Eric, our firstborn, came out of the womb with an attitude that said, "Don't you tell me what to do!" Right from the beginning, our will became pitted against his and many difficulties ensued. Having a child who seemed angry and upset a great deal of the time was not how we imagined our family life. We were distraught, and the advice we got from those around us, or from the books we read, did not help. To get the wisdom we were seeking we had to listen to another source.

One day, when Eric was almost two years old, I returned home from my teaching day and Margie said, "An amazing thing happened today while I was reading *Green Eggs and Ham* to Eric." Reading books over and over to him was part of the usual routine we believed would enrich his life. She continued, "I got to the part where the guy who is being pursued turns to the guy who has been pursuing him and says, 'Sam you let me be,' and Eric stopped me. He looked up at me and said, 'Mom, you let me be.'"

We talked a lot about the meaning of the message this little guy had given us. It began our thinking very differently about control and its effect on our family. The learning and changes that resulted continued for years. The more we understood about control, resistance and rebellion, and the more we were able to let go of the many seemingly almost automatic attempts to have control over him, the better our relationship with him became.

Attentively listening to our children taught us more about child raising than any books we had read. For example, before we had children, we had decided that we would never hit our children, and we never did. But when we got frustrated and wanted our way, we yelled a lot. One day, when Josh was about two years old, I was upset and yelled at him. He looked up at me and with a tear rolling down his cheek said, "Daddy, when you yell at me, I think I'm gonna die."

Back to the drawing board. Maybe yelling was as harmful as hitting after all. We learned that, if we were determined to preserve our children's integrity, we had to learn to deal with our upsets in ways that did not disrespect them. We also learned if we wanted to teach them to deal with their own upsets in respectful ways, that we had to model that behavior.

I can't say I never yelled again, but every time I did the image of little Josh with a tear in his eye came to my mind. I knew I was the one with the problem, and it was I who needed to do something about myself.

If you ask children how they feel they may not tell you, but to know what a child feels all you really have to do is remember your own feelings in similar situations from your own past. To feel compassion we often must be able to put ourselves into other people's shoes. Unfortunately, due to our ability to repress painful moments, we often forget how it felt being the recipient of a bigger person's anger. This is the focus the next teaching story.

TEACHING STORY #4

My Other Two Are Angels, But Oh That Third One!

Differences, Disconnection, and Struggle

Andrea and Bert had been unhappy for some time and were talking about separating when she got pregnant with their third child. The months before the birth were tumultuous, and when Davy was three months old Bert left and had was never heard from again.

For the past six years, Andrea had been juggling the responsibilities of a full-time job and finishing her bachelor's begree, along with the additional demands of being a single parent. The pressure was taking its toll and she found herself exploding in anger more frequently than she liked.

All the kids tiptoed around, trying to avoid upsetting Mom, but it was Davy who just couldn't seem to stay out of trouble. Davy had always been a rather free-spirited daredevil who often seemed to border on being completely out of control. Andrea tried to manage him as best she could.

Then, one day, a day like many others, her pressure-filled workday ended as she absent-mindedly moved the computer cursor and clicked "shut down." She shoved some papers in her briefcase and threw good-byes to her office mates as she briskly traveled the familiar route to the parking lot.

A quick stop at the market and she was on the road home. Turning into her driveway, the day's tensions momentarily drained from her body and she swelled with pride over more than her neatly appointed house.

The three reasons for her joy greeted her in their own unique way. She opened the door and her packages and knees hit the floor simultaneously as Davy ran into her arms. The tickle that coursed through her body caused a delicious shudder of pleasure, and she thought, "He is so damn cute."

In the same instant, Darren shouted, "Hi, Mom!" from the cockpit of his airplane as he practiced landings on his computer flight simulator. Meanwhile, Geneva waved a warm hello while indicating with her index finger that she would be right off the phone.

Unloading her groceries, Andrea thought, "What great kids." Darren, a senior in high school, was rather shy and seemed to lose himself for hours on the computer. Although he didn't show his feelings, Andrea had noticed tears in his eyes at times when she had yelled at Davy. Then she'd see his deep sensitivity as he made some contact with Davy, whether touching him on the head or comforting him with a smile.

Geneva, a year younger than Darren, was maturing into quite a young woman. Blessed with a great personality and a quick mind, she was on the fast track to success. As Andrea started preparing dinner she meditated on her daily mantra: "I'm so lucky. I'm so lucky."

Within two minutes, however, Geneva still had not gotten off the phone to fulfill her dinner responsibilities, and Davy was bugging his sister by turning up the volume on the television. After a few unsuccessful attempts to gain some peace, Geneva yelled, "Mom, would you please tell him to turn down the TV!"

Andrea donned her peacemaker hat. "Davy, come in here for a minute. Geneva, I really could use some help."

Davy threw his sister a petulant look of disdain. Slowly, he made his way into the kitchen, whining contemptuously, "Why do I have to stop watching my program just because she's got to talk to her boyfriend?"

While standing at the sink rinsing and admiring the fresh head of lettuce she had just purchased, Andrea calmly tried explaining things to Davy. With her back toward him, she never noticed his eyes rolling back in his head and his face screwing-up in boredom as he slowly inched his way back toward the living room.

When Andrea realized she had been talking to herself, she slammed the spigot shut and, glowering through narrowed eyes, she barked, "Young man, come back here this minute!"

Davy paid no heed and Andrea snapped. She chased after him and in her frustration gave him a hard smack across his bottom. Davy ran to his room crying. Andrea yelled at Geneva, "Get off that damn phone this minute and get in here! I need help!"

The house, a moment ago bustling with good energy, plunged into an eerie, strained quiet. Davy, feeling picked on and angry, defiantly sniffled in his room. Geneva, fighting to deny the tension in her body, whispered a hurried good-bye to her boyfriend. Darren burrowed even deeper into cyberspace. Andrea despondently peeled the potatoes.

Andrea and Davy had survived many rounds of these interactions, but now they were occurring more frequently. Davy was becoming more obstreperous at home and at school. Andrea was suffering growing doubts about her worth and her ability to love. Added to the burden of her life was the weight of a never-ending series of school conferences on the subject of "What to do with Davy." Although she consciously didn't know it, she intuitively knew that the only answer she would get—"Send him to a therapist"—would only add both to her financial burden and to Davy's self-doubts.

Davy had become the family's "identified patient," the one who was at fault and needed to be "fixed." He was beginning to believe and act out the labels of "bad" and "slow learner" that were being attached to him. He felt unloved and unlovable and was withdrawing into his protective shell more of the time.

The interactions in the house simulated the repeated pattern of human history—war, periods between wars euphemistically called peace, followed by another war. Without knowing how to achieve real peace, Andrea found the uneasy periods between wars like waiting for the other shoe to drop.

During their battles, Andrea's physical punishment of Davy had never gone beyond a few slaps on his behind, but both sides ominously sensed the approaching Armageddon when she would "lose it" and not stop.

The stress was taking its toll in every area of Andrea's life. Lately, she had missed more classes than she would have liked and had turned in work far below her capabilities. One evening in school, her teacher said to her at the break, "Can you stay for a few minutes after class?"

She immediately locked into fear and uttered a faint, "Sure."

Her fear that her teacher was upset with her proved to be false. Instead, he gently counseled her, "I notice you're more distracted lately and I miss your contributions in class. If there's anything I can do to help, please let me know."

"Thanks a lot, Mr. Haley. I was afraid you were angry with me."

"Andrea, I'm sorry I didn't make it clearer at the break that I was just concerned. I know you must be under a lot of pressure, and I certainly don't want to add to your burden."

Andrea started crying and Mr. Haley tenderly comforted her. She briefly shared with him what was going on and ended with "I just feel not only like I can't handle everything, but that it's just going to keep getting worse."

"I hear how overwhelmed you are and it sounds like you don't have much support. Can I make a suggestion?"

"Sure, I'm open to anything."

"I hope what I'm going to say doesn't offend you, but are you involved with any kind of spiritual discipline?"

"No. I stopped going to church a long time ago."

"Well, there's a very different kind of church in town. It's called the Center for Positive Living. It's hard to describe because it's not like any church I've ever been to. I've been going there for about a year and it's made a big difference in my life. If you're ever interested in going, just let me know."

"Thanks," Andrea replied with a mixed response of excitement and apprehension.

"You seem a little hesitant."

"Well, Mr. Haley, to tell you the truth, I guess I'm a little shy in new situations," she said, her color rising.

He answered with an assuring smile. "If it will make it easier, we can meet before the service and I'll introduce you around. But you'll have to stop calling me Mr. Haley. I prefer John."

"Thanks, Mr. Ha, . . . sorry, John. It sounds great. How about this Sunday?"

"Great. I'll meet you at the corner of Taylor and Main at 9:45."

The Sunday service exceeded John's positive description. Reverend Toni was energetic and upbeat. Contrary to Andrea's childhood experiences at church, the people seem thrilled to be there, and the music lifted her spirits. In her sermon, Reverend Toni talked about modern-day pressures and single parenting. She related it to passages in the Bible and her own struggles. Andrea felt like she was talking directly to her.

At the end of the sermon, Reverend Toni announced a six-week series of classes starting the following month called "Loving Parenting." At the conclusion of the service, Andrea immediately signed up. On the drive home she felt like a huge weight had been lifted from her shoulders.

Heart Learning

Sharon, a trained psychologist who was also studying to become a minister, taught the class. Andrea learned many lessons during the series, but even more helpful was the support group that formed to deepen their learning about what Sharon referred to as "The most important and most difficult job we will ever undertake."

Sharon introduced a perspective that Andrea had never heard or read about until that day. She opened the class by saying, "Rather than trying to find better ways to get our children to change, which only perpetuates the problems that arise from power struggles and seeing themselves as wrong and 'the problem,' we're going to focus on what we, as parents, need to learn to become more loving to our children and to ourselves.

"This will not only be helpful for you, it will take a huge burden off them and help them feel better about themselves. As their self-esteem rises, they can learn new ways of behaving that will better meet their needs and your own. For you, it will mean learning the many lessons that will allow compassion, for yourself and for them, to be active more of the time. It is, I believe, a spiritual approach to child raising."

Through the class, Andrea discovered that underneath her anger lay a cacophony of feelings she was afraid to acknowledge. Over-burdened by the responsibilities she had assumed, she was confused about how to deal with them and was afraid she was incapable of handling it all. She felt responsible for her failed marriage and guilty for blaming Davy. She feared that if she allowed herself to feel sad-ness, pain, and anger, her feelings would overwhelm her and she would be unable to fulfill her responsibilities. She felt alone, unseen, and on the edge of a nervous breakdown.

Her guilt and blame kept her from feeling compassion for herself. Without self-compassion, she believed that to keep it together she had to "steel herself" to stay in control. As a consequence she could not feel compassion for Davy. Without such compassion her self-es-teem was continually being eroded.

In her diary, she kept a growing list of what she missed when she lost her compassion for Davy. The following was on her list:

When I lose compassion for Davy I fail to:

1. See the intense sadness and fear behind his eyes as he cow-ers in front of me, the person whose love and acceptance is so important to him.
2. Understand that his behavior is motivated by very important reasons, not the least of which is his need to establish his own identity.
3. Remember the pain I felt as a child when my parents harshly censored me.
4. Feel my deep love for him and allow my motherly love to nurture him.

The bottom line is that when I fail him, I fail myself.

Andrea learned that when Davy misbehaved, for her to respond with nurturing she would have to see beyond his behavior. Another page in her diary was devoted to that idea:

When Davy misbehaves, there is a very good possibility that any of the following may be primarily responsible:

1. The little guy may have come to believe that he is a burden and is responsible for my difficulties.

2. He is caught between his need for my approval and his need for his own identity. When he resists my demands he is acting out his confusion.
3. He feels alone, unseen, and scared. He is hungry to be touched but does not know it, nor how to ask for it.

As Andrea understood more about the struggle inside Davy and gained more compassion for both herself and him, she was able to respond more of the time with love and nurturing.

As her learning continued, cracks in her exterior image exposed her inner feelings of sadness, helplessness, and loneliness. She had to acknowledge that although she was strong and capable, she needed help and caring from her kids. Her past efforts to get those needs met, a smorgasbord of demands that included ordering, punishment, threats, and guilt, had only served to wear her out and to alienate them. As a result, she had come to doubt that the kids really cared about her. Admitting to those doubts was a big first step; testing them out was next.

The overwhelming odds were that her kids really did care, and when they saw their mom vulnerable and needing help, they would probably respond with love. She could then get the kind of caring that would help her release some of the burden of feeling responsible and needing to be in control of everything. She didn't know that, because all she had seen was their attempts to avoid the responsibilities she had been trying to impose on them. To give up her tough outer shell and stand emotionally naked before her children would leave her very vulnerable and that was terrifying to her.

Through her learning, Andrea developed many sources from which she received support, including: the positive messages at church services and events; readings and classes that deepened her ability to stay connected to her compassion; the ongoing group of parents that served as a resource for each other; and friendships with people like John. One additional source of support that she discovered later in her story was totally unexpected.

Being Your Own Hero, Fulfilling Connections and Possibilities

As her relationship with herself improved, Andrea's life took on a very different look. At 4:59 p.m., with her day's work done, a fleeting thought of the evening she was about to spend with her kids sent a smile throughout her entire body. Although she had many things on her plate, the kids taking some of the responsibility for household chores, including shopping for food and sometimes even making dinner, had made her evenings at home much more relaxed and enjoyable.

This was not easily achieved. Of the many things Andrea learned that helped improve her relationship with the kids, the idea that had the greatest impact was compassionate listening. As each family member became better able to hear each other more considerately, they shared more of their thoughts, feelings, and concerns.

Their family meetings were so satisfying that they eagerly looked forward to having regularly scheduled time together. In this environment of trust and caring came a workable plan for how the chores would be divided. And even when differences arose, they were able to get through them fairly quickly. This had a profound effect on each of them.

Having the space and learning valuable skills for communication encouraged Darren to emerge from his self-imposed shadows. He assumed more responsibility and with it gained more personal power. Part of his new role was to become more involved with Davy. Having someone other than Mom helping to fulfill his needs for nurturing and connection helped Davy become a much more pleasant person to be with.

It is also important to note that in the Andrea's support group, one of the other parents related her own son's problems to those of Davy. She suggested that her son's dyslexia had contributed greatly to his behavioral problems. Upon having Davy tested, it was discovered that although he was not dyslexic, he did suffer from biochemical imbalances that affected his mood. He continued to be tested until the proper medication and dosage was found. However, just knowing that his interior drives were not merely psychological changed how everyone saw him, and being treated respectfully helped him feel better about himself.

The family meetings also uncovered the need each child felt to have quality time with their mom. They came up with a plan that called for Andrea to spend time alone with each child two hours each week. How that time was spent was to be determined half of the time by the child and half by Andrea.

Darren spent his time teaching his mom to play video games. Andrea did her best to develop an interest in something that seemed so far from anything she had found enjoyable. She was astounded to discover that she could grow to enjoy something that seemed out of the question only a few short months ago. Now, whether they were chasing each other through the various perils of a computer game or cruising the Internet, they had a good time laughing and playing.

For her time with Darren, Andrea loved to watch and talk about films that were important to her. Darren called them "chick flicks," but in spite of himself, they opened him to new dimensions of himself. Discussing films like *Antonio's Line* and *Joy Luck Club* helped him gain a greater appreciation of women's issues and become more comfortable with women and the feminine side of himself. Andrea was delighted and touched that she had found ways to share and feel closer with Darren.

Davy had always loved building and playing with his toys, but now there was an added dimension to his play. Getting down on the floor and playing with him freed Andrea to be more spontaneous. Sometimes, on the spur of the moment, they would begin crawling around in a game of tag or just allow themselves to blend rhythmically into a game she dubbed "touch and nuzzle."

Andrea loved reading to Davy. Part of their time was spent going to the library to find books. The best part of reading together for both of them, however, was having him cuddled on her lap.

One night it was Geneva's special evening for "time alone with Mom." Geneva and Andrea now loved to take walks and to allow whatever emerged to become the topic of their conversation. On this evening, just as they were about to take their walk, Davy and Geneva got into one of their sibling power struggles.

Geneva was talking on the phone and Davy was bugging her. Andrea tried to intercede, but Davy was bound and determined to get his sister's goat. Geneva cupped her hand over the receiver and yelled at Davy, "You little shit, why don't you go play with your dolls?"

Davy was stung by the put-down impugning his masculinity. With the full force of his fury and through a mountain of tears, he lunged at Geneva. Andrea felt her anger boil. As she started to pull Davy off Geneva, she remembered the "list," and that beneath his behavior there was a hurting little boy. Instead of yelling, her heart opened and she gathered Davy in her arms.

At first he resisted, but soon he collapsed sobbing in her arms. Propped against an old trunk filled with toys, she sat on the floor gently rocking him. His tears touched off her own childhood memories of the pain and deprivation of being alone, unseen, and scared, and her body returned to that time long ago.

Davy looked up at her and their eyes locked. He tenderly brushed a tear from her cheek and gave her a hug that said, "I love you." This special moment would always remain as a segment on her "Life Highlights" reel.

Later, as she and Geneva walked in the nearby park discussing the earlier interaction, Andrea again felt tears welling up. Geneva sensed her mom's distress and said, "Mom, why don't we sit down for a minute?"

Geneva put her arm around Andrea, and Andrea sank into Geneva's nurturing aura. Feeling safe in her daughter's love, she allowed the floodgate of both her past and her present pain to open, releasing a torrent of tears.

Geneva also took the opportunity to talk about her reactions to Davy. Feeling both her pain and his, she committed herself to making amends when they returned home, if he was still awake.

As they silently continued their walk hand in hand, Andrea imperceptibly shook her head in disbelief as she thought, "It seems like only yesterday that this sixteen-year-old was my baby. Now, she has not only grown into a woman, she is becoming my best friend."

Geneva's face glowed with a satisfied smile as she lightly squeezed her mom's hand. Giving comfort to her mother opened the nurturing side of Geneva that she would grow to really love.

Andrea knew that she had come a long way on the journey toward becoming more loving to herself and others. She also knew that there was a lot more to learn. As she kept on learning and gaining the confidence she needed to remain more open and loving, the chances were excellent that everyone around her would continue to respond more lovingly, and parenting would be more of the joy it can to be.

Getting What We Want With Our Children

Most of us want our kids to be happy, responsible, and successful, and our families to be close and joyful. Yet even with sincere effort we may not realize our dreams. Parents and children often seem more like adversaries than good friends, living in war zones rather than sanctuaries. The typical dismay of distraught parents over unhappy, uncommunicative, rebellious, and irresponsible kids is a direct result of an environment in which disrespectful behavior has led to low trust.

Many negative consequences follow an unsafe environment. For example, a telling symptom of low trust is people keeping their innermost thoughts and feelings to themselves or lying about them. Since this is typically true with mates and employees, why should we expect anything different from our children? The fact that 90 percent of teenagers lie to their parents, as reported in a year 2000 study by the Jacobson Institute for Ethics and Meaning, should give us pause to consider the kind of environment we are creating.

Since Fulfilling Connections depend on the faith that allows us to let go of control, this is the premier challenge of parenting. If you thought letting go of control was scary with your adult partner, fear goes off the charts with children. Parenting presents us with many possible pitfalls that we desperately want to avoid, such as being a failure in our own eyes and in the eyes of others, and that in keeping our hearts open, we will not take good care of our own needs. These fears, and many others, come into play as we try to get our children to learn in school and do their homework, get enough sleep, and behave and dress in appropriate ways, including being nice to others.

But, there is one fear that far outstrips all others. The most terrifying fear of parenting is the possibility that our child could die. Much of trying to control children falls into the category of trying to protect them from physical harm. Although very understandable, the set of dynamics that results when we attempt to have control over our children usually brings about a whole host of difficulties.

Thus, parenting gives us nonstop opportunities to test our faith. When our faith fails, attempts at control communicate that we lack faith in our children. Communicating that we have faith in their ability to create their own sense of well-being translates into not worrying excessively or avoiding overprotection. Such faith nurtures and empowers both child and parent and leaves us free to be fully present in the field of Fulfilling Connections. The following is an account of one of my own tests of faith.

From the time Eric was three years old he had wanted to drive. Every moment he was in the car he studiously watched my movements, practicing in his mind how to shift and steer. The day he got his learner's permit, we went to an empty lot and he flawlessly performed every aspect of driving. Needless to say, on the morning of his sixteenth birthday we were the first people in line at the Department of Motor Vehicles to get his driver's license. I had no qualms about Eric's skills. My squeamishness was not to be felt until later that day.

For weeks Eric had been planning a spring skiing trip with a couple of friends to Mammoth Mountain. Margie and I had tried to discourage him by telling him of the possible dangers of such a trip, but he would have none of it. She and I discussed the possibility of just forbidding him to go. We knew that being authoritarian would result in family turmoil, but maybe this was one of those times when our comfort level was more important than his was.

Finally, we decided to bite the bullet. We expressed our fears for his safety and assured him that the fears were not about his ability but about our own fear of something bad happening to him. I asked him to indulge his concerned parents and call every hour or so. He laughed at my feeble attempt at humor and said, "I'll call you when we get there."

Standing at the front door watching the left turn indicator blinking as his (my) car disappeared from sight, my stomach started to do somersaults. I spent the next five hours alternatively gripping the armrests of my chair and working in the yard as I fantasized his death and my guilt over letting him go. Finally, came the blessed moment of the phone call informing me that Eric had arrived safely. I collapsed in a pool of perspiration.

I thought a lot about all the internal turmoil I could have avoided by just putting my foot down. But I also considered that my son would have resisted my attempts to control him, interpreted my behavior not as caring but as a lack of trust in him, and that there would have been many unpleasant repercussions. I also knew that my fears for Eric's safety were probably groundless, and that since the day he learned to walk I had had fears of his independence.

I realized that my own fears of losing him and of him getting hurt were part of the contract I had made when I allowed myself to love him. I recognized that even if my worst fears were to come true (God forbid), I could survive my pain and eventually thrive. I understood how often parents are tested to see if we can love and guide our children without controlling them. Many times I had not passed the test, but this time I was proud that I had.

The real challenge of parenting is how to keep our hearts open and respond to difficulties, disappointment, and unmet expectations with an open heart; how to teach our children to be responsible; and how to discipline them in ways that do not compromise either their integrity or our own. There are not many models to show us what respectful parenting looks like. Most examples from our families of origin, movies, and television demonstrate only authoritarian or permissive responses, neither of which come from an open heart.

Power Over or Power With

It is so easy to use our power over our children. We are stronger, more intellectually adept, and have financial resources they do not. But if we use our power over them, we are teaching them that it is okay to use their own power to control others. It then stands to reason that when they get into positions of power they will not have learned any other way and will justify their own use of power.

Typically, child rearing is a graphic example of using Power Over. Children are routinely manipulated and humiliated by their parents and older siblings, who use their superior size, independence, or verbal ability to take advantage of a child's need for love. It has been done to all of us and we as parents have all, at times, used it on our children. We are not bad people for doing or having done these things; we are merely frightened and unaware.

A stark contrast can be seen in the way parents use either Power Over or Power With to handle the universal difficulties that arise with children including everyday concerns like school work, allowance, chores, bedtime, discipline, watching television, or major traumas that involve relocating, having another child, or putting a pet to sleep.

In the Power Over model, parents impose their beliefs about appropriate behavior on their children. The child's feelings and thoughts are usually not heard, and as a result children rarely feel considered. In the Power With model, the expression of a child's feelings is met with compassionate listening. Even if you have considered your child's feelings, unless the child expresses them, he or she will not feel heard.

For example, suppose you have an opportunity for an advancement that requires moving to another city. You may have engaged in many hours of conversation with your spouse considering his or her feelings. Once the decision is made you tell your children. But they have many feelings which need to be expressed, including their fears of moving to a new city, going to a new school, making new friends, their sadness over leaving their old friends, their anger about having this decision imposed on them or being left out of the decision-making process, which may have taken place in whispers or behind closed doors. These are the feelings they need to be heard and acknowledged.

Children in this situation do not need to be talked out of their feelings by being told that everything is going to be all right, that they will make new friends, or what a wonderful opportunity this is. Such assurance will just increase their disconnected feelings. They just need to be listened to compassionately, to feel heard, and to know that their feelings are important and have been considered. The decision may go against what they want, but they, like each of us, are better able to handle things not going their way when they feel heard and understood. That is what makes us feel loved and connected to others.

Taking a look through the lens of Power Over or Power With regarding discipline is particularly relevant and illuminating. Without Heart Feelings, disciplining children (and others) is an exercise in being right, making a point, trying to force adherence to rules, and maintaining dominance. With these things being more important than compassion, the feelings and rights of those being disciplined become abrogated. The results lie in the typical responses that occur when people feel unseen, uncared for, and disrespected, such as resistance, rebellion, and irresponsibility. A typical result for the disciplinarian is the anxiety, tension, and burden of having to maintain the watchful vigil of a policeman. A typical result for the relationship is the distance that occurs when people disconnect from their Heart Feelings.

When an upsetting event occurs with a child and compassion is center stage, an appropriate solution, which may or may not include some form of punishment, will be found. Remembering our own humiliation when we were disciplined without compassion fuels a commitment not to subject our own children to that experience. Compassionate discipline asks us to remember:

- Our own strong need as a child for our individuality, even at the cost of making mistakes, and to respect that in our child
- To include our child in whatever solution is decided upon
- Not to take things so seriously and have faith that our children have the capability to work things out for themselves. With that attitude we can play with even the most serious situations without handling them frivolously

You can ask yourself, before, during, and after disciplining your child: "Do I feel like holding my child, and does he or she feel like being held by me?" If the answer is no, you have discovered an important direction for learning more about compassionate discipline. Again, difficulties doing these things are merely more opportunities for Heart Learning.

The "Paths Through Conflict" chart on page 130 for parents is included in *Do I Have to Give Up Me to Be Loved by My Kids?* The Path of Unloving Behavior reflects a disconnection from our hearts and The Path of Loving Behavior reflects a heart connection.

Applying the Paths Through Conflict Chart

To illustrate using "The Paths Through Conflict" chart, a conflict over finding out that your teenage child has been smoking marijuana will be used.

Your immediate response might be on the left side of the chart as anger accompanied by some kind of punishment or lecture. If you have ever faced that situation, you know full well the futility and negative consequences of that reaction.

Closing your heart and becoming an authoritarian dispensing discipline or information takes you away from your compassion and learning and creates separation between you and him. Without an openhearted connection, even a well-intentioned disciplinary measure is hit or miss, with a much better chance of missing. Any action on your part, which is motivated by an intent to change him, will only perpetuate his troubling behavior, as well as the disconnection both from himself and from you. Anything that produces disconnection is not nurturing.

But what if you saw deeply into this human being in front of you, past his behavior and into what was driving the behavior? What if you saw a struggling person tied into a bundle of fears, unsure about his attractiveness, ability to make friends, sexuality, intelligence, social skills, and future? What if you remembered the full impact of the confusion and self-doubt you went through as a teenager? How would you respond?

Sometimes advice may be appropriate, but not always. Sometimes imposing limits or what has been called "tough love," or offering to send him to a psychologist may be appropriate, but not always. So how do you know what is nurturing?

Nurturing with Heart Feelings requires putting aside what you think is appropriate and connecting with the person. In this instance, it would mean having enough compassion for your son to get beyond his behavior to find out what is driving that behavior. Then, your course of action would come from an informed and heart-connected place.

THE PATHS THROUGH CONFLICT

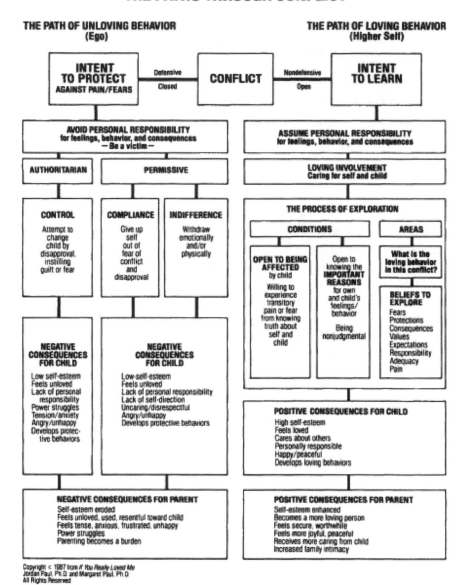

THE PATH OF UNLOVING BEHAVIOR
(Ego)

THE PATH OF LOVING BEHAVIOR
(Higher Self)

| INTENT TO PROTECT AGAINST PAIN/FEARS | Defensive / Closed → CONFLICT ← Nondefensive / Open | INTENT TO LEARN |

AVOID PERSONAL RESPONSIBILITY
for feelings, behavior, and consequences
— Be a victim —

ASSUME PERSONAL RESPONSIBILITY
for feelings, behavior, and consequences

AUTHORITARIAN | **PERMISSIVE**

LOVING INVOLVEMENT
Caring for self and child

CONTROL
Attempt to change child by disapproval, instilling guilt or fear

COMPLIANCE
Give up self out of fear of conflict and disapproval

INDIFFERENCE
Withdraw emotionally and/or physically

THE PROCESS OF EXPLORATION

CONDITIONS | **AREAS**

OPEN TO BEING AFFECTED by child
Willing to experience transitory pain or fear from knowing truth about self and child

Open to knowing the **IMPORTANT REASONS** for own and child's feelings/behavior

Being nonjudgmental

What is the loving behavior in this conflict?

BELIEFS TO EXPLORE
Fears
Protections
Consequences
Values
Expectations
Responsibility
Adequacy
Pain

NEGATIVE CONSEQUENCES FOR CHILD
Low self-esteem
Feels unloved
Lack of personal responsibility
Power struggles
Tension/anxiety
Angry/unhappy
Develops protective behaviors

NEGATIVE CONSEQUENCES FOR CHILD
Low self-esteem
Feels unloved
Lack of personal responsibility
Lack of self-direction
Uncaring/disrespectful
Angry/unhappy
Develops protective behaviors

POSITIVE CONSEQUENCES FOR CHILD
High self-esteem
Feels loved
Cares about others
Personally responsible
Happy/peaceful
Develops loving behaviors

NEGATIVE CONSEQUENCES FOR PARENT
Self-esteem eroded
Feels unloved, used, resentful toward child
Feels tense, anxious, frustrated, unhappy
Power struggles
Parenting becomes a burden

POSITIVE CONSEQUENCES FOR PARENT
Self-esteem enhanced
Becomes a more loving person
Feels secure, worthwhile
Feels more joyful, peaceful
Receives more caring from child
Increased family intimacy

A teenager who has been discovered to be taking drugs needs what we all need:

1. To feel connected to others by feeling their compassion, and the caring, concern, valuing, acceptance, and understanding which follow naturally
2. To receive help connecting to his own Heart Feelings. To be nurturing, your heart must be open to him.

An intent to learn about yourself would take you into all the issues that have already been discussed in this book related to the fears and Disconnecting Beliefs that block your Heart Feelings.

Making Fulfilling Connections a Priority

When an intent to make Heart Feelings an important and integral part of family life, any activity is an opportunity for Fulfilling Connections, and family life goes through major changes.

For example, at mealtimes, talking about impersonal things would be secondary to learning about those at the table on a deeper level. Discussions about how you are feeling about your lives and your real concerns would hold sway over criticism, arguments, and dispassionate chronologies about the day's events. Although typical dinner table discussions seem much safer, they rarely meet the need for Fulfilling Connections and often become experiences to be avoided. Conversations that are honest and personal connect us to our love for each other and ourselves. They may be intellectual discussions that lead to new discoveries and awareness, intimate personal sharing, or learning about what blocks us from our Heart Feelings.

Typical conversation subjects like sports, weather, food, gossip, and stories about past events do not meet these criteria. There is nothing wrong or bad about spending time in discussions where there is no Heart Learning, but they will not energize and satisfy you like meaningful (meaning-full) discussions that involve being touched with important personal learning, and feeling seen, heard, and appreciated.

Television, typically an alienating and isolating experience, can produce Fulfilling Connections when sitting together is a time for physical, as well as emotional, touch. Some of the programs watched would then be chosen based on their relationship to developing and integrating Heart

Feelings into our abilities. Parents and young children might watch *Mr. Rogers' Neighborhood* and older children and adults might enjoy watching *Any Day Now*. These programs could then be the subjects of discussions about what effect they had on the viewer and what might be learned from them.

Homework, probably the greatest source of family strife, is one of the hardest areas for parents to have faith that the desire to learn is internally motivated. And yet, the problems around homework very often are a result of a control issue that has created a power struggle.

When children resist being controlled, they do it in an area that is important to their parents. In small children, evidence of a power struggle can be seen in bedwetting or a refusal to eat "appropriately." In older children, if schoolwork is important to parents and a child needs to take a stand for his or her independence, homework often becomes the battleground. The unspoken statement by the child is "I'll show you that you can't force me to conform to your way of thinking." The child may not even consciously know that not doing well in school is a rebellion.

Letting go of control and acting with an open heart means allowing children to do poorly, or even fail, and suffer the consequences of his of her actions, *while deeply caring for the difficulties they are encountering*. Trying to coerce children or allowing them to fail without keeping an open heart is either authoritarian or permissive. Neither feels like caring to a child because neither comes with an open heart.

Attempting to break a power struggle with an older child is much more problematic than when a child is younger. First of all, the power struggle is much more deeply engrained, and second, the consequences of failure are much greater. Doing poorly, or even failing, in the second grade is much less problematic than doing poorly or failing in high school.

Even traditions and rituals go through a major transformation when Heart Feelings are a priority. When parents feel strictly adhering to a set of predetermined rules becomes paramount, Heart Feelings take a back seat. When this adherence is related to a ritual, openness to learning about the ritual itself and the effect it has on the lives of the participants gets lost. Issues such as caring, respect, and relevance may not be given much consideration. Fulfilling Connections become mortally wounded and result in passive involvement (being there in body but not spirit), boredom, lack of interest, or avoiding the experience whenever possible.

The Agony and the Ecstasy of Heart Learning with Children

Opening to Heart Learning puts you on the roller coaster of feelings. For example, consider the following situation that occurred between my daughter and me.

Although the separation of her parents had been her mother's decision, I felt Sheryl was angry with me for causing the split. Her indifference and detachment left me with an aching emptiness and an incredible sadness. Feeling at a loss as to how to recapture our old relationship, I found myself calling her less and less frequently.

I had always felt very close to Sheryl, and certainly she was handling the tumultuous changes in the only way she knew how, but it hurt me deeply. Occasionally I got up my nerve to ask her about the obvious strain between us. This was inevitably met with irritation or reticence on her part. That's why her late night call surprised me.

I waited, somewhat guarded, to see what she had on her mind. After a few minutes of idle chitchat she said, "I have something to tell you. This is really difficult, but I just can't keep it in any longer."

She paused and I waited, intuitively dreading her words. Finally, she said, "I have never felt loved by you."

It felt as if a dagger had been thrust into my stomach. The first words that formed and I choked back were "How could you say that? You have always been my little darling. After having three sons I treasured you beyond words! Who took you to your gymnastics lessons and never missed a meet? Who read you stories? Who was with you every night to say together the night time ritual you made up: 'Good night, sleep tight, and I love you sooooo very much that I'd have to say "very" for my whole life, and when I'm dead God will say it for me?'"

All these thoughts wanted a voice, but I knew better than to throw them up all over her. Regardless of what was true for me or how much the accusation stung, I knew that what she was saying felt true for her and that I had to honestly hear her. I forced myself to swallow my defensiveness and said, "That really hurts, but tell me more about why you feel that way."

I could hear the breath she had been holding in anticipation of my denial, defense, and outrage release. "I always felt a distance between us," she said. "I don't quite understand it. Even though you were always around, and were physically there to take care of me, I never felt an emotional closeness. Do you know what I'm talking about?"

Almost inaudibly, through the sadness that had constricted my throat, I said, "I think I do, sweetheart. I've been learning a lot about myself since your mom and I separated, but I think my most profound learning is around who I really am. I've been so disconnected from my heart most of my life that it's been almost impossible to really connect with anyone else. So it's no wonder you didn't feel my love. I feel awful about that."

We cried deeply together. Each time either of us began to say anything we broke down again. Finally she said she felt better, and that perhaps we should end the conversation. I mumbled something like, "Are we having fun yet?" and with the tension broken, we both started laughing.

As I drifted off to sleep that night, I knew that although there was still a great deal of healing to be done, my daughter and I had made a breakthrough that now gave us the chance to develop the kind of relationship for which we each had hungered. That night I slept peacefully with feelings of fulfillment and hope.

Ideally, I would like to have the profound opportunity to parent my children again from the emotional place I am in today. They deserved to have the best of me and they got that far too infrequently. As I've said before, given my fears and lack of information, I was always doing the best I could at the time. So I don't feel guilty, but I do feel sad—sad for all the wonderful experiences we missed as a family and I missed with each of them.

These days, we are having more and more Fulfilling Connections, and I'm really grateful for that. My most fervent wish for all parents and children is to have more Fulfilling Connections. It's what makes my children the greatest gift that Spirit has given to me.

Chapter Seven

Open Hearts At Work

If we don't change our direction we'll end up where we're headed.
—Ancient Chinese saying

This chapter addresses two work-related areas. First, we examine the work environment and how it can be used as an important tool in becoming powerful. Second, we will look at connecting your heart to what you do.

The chapter begins with the last teaching story. Alex is a business executive. Even though the situations he confronts may not be ones that you are dealing with, the challenges he faces in keeping his heart open and becoming more powerful are universal. As you read the story, try relating what Alex is learning to any situation in which you are a "leader," in your work group or family, with the team you coach, or with your customers.

TEACHING STORY #5

He's A Nice Guy, But Don't Cross Him

Differences, Disconnection, and Struggle

Slumped in his chair, Alex felt overwhelmed and impotent, feelings that have never before been part of his storybook life. Born not only with a silver spoon in his mouth, but also with a powerful internal motivation to succeed, his life had seemed charmed.

Achieving academic honors, being elected to many prestigious student body positions, and, while on his way to getting an MBA from Harvard, garnering All-American honors in volleyball were all

---

taken in stride. Even meeting Jane read like a passage from a romantic novella: "The short ride from the ski patrol hut to the hospital emergency room was like a surreal dream. As he lay motionless, his broken leg in a makeshift splint, a beautiful blonde strode in, gave him a perfunctory 'Hello,' put down her clipboard, and went about examining his leg. Satisfied that he was being well taken care of, she took two steps toward the head of the bed, their eyes met, and everything around them blurred into insignificance."

Soon after Jane finished her internship, they were married. Jane went to work part-time at a nearby hospital, while devoting most of her time to raising their son, Peter. Alex, at thirty-one, became sales manager for a rapidly growing mid-size electronics company. His customary hard work, combined with his talent and good fortune, made it inevitable that he would become the youngest vice-president in the company's history.

Even with his success, however, he never lost the down-to-earth manner that made him so popular. Alex's congeniality served him well both in sales and in his limited supervisory roles. But the added responsibilities of being sales manager, and the internal problems that were rampant within his company, brought him face to face with issues that could not be resolved with a glad-hand and words of encouragement.

Alex started drowning in the sheer numbers of people in turmoil. Of particular concern were territorial issues causing serious distrust on the sales team, along with a support staff who felt unappreciated. The resulting high burnout and increasing turnover rate became the focus of more and more staff meetings.

Alex decided to confer with Joe, an old friend he had met in graduate school. Although there was a fifteen-year age difference between them, Alex and Joe had become good friends. Joe had returned to school for his MBA after successfully building two start-up electronics companies that had been merged into larger conglomerates. With his financial future secure, his goal had shifted to helping entrepreneurs build their own companies.

While in school, Joe became a valuable mentor to Alex in the organizational and financial aspects of business. They didn't talk much about personal issues since that was not of interest for Alex. Although they had lost touch in the seven years since graduation, when Alex realized he was in trouble there was no one else he even considered calling.

Joe had stayed in school longer than Alex because his interest in people drew him to classes and seminars on the "softer" side of business. In business school, psychology was often the butt of many jokes, but that didn't deter Joe. Exploring the human condition was fascinating to him.

Upon leaving school, Joe was content to specialize his management consulting practice only with those CEOs and upper-level managers who were interested in a bigger picture than just "the bottom line." He always thought about business as having a double bottom line—profits and people.

During their brief telephone exchange, Alex laid out a well-organized synopsis of the difficulties he was encountering. Even though Joe knew that Alex did not know of the narrow focus his consulting business had assumed, he had such good feelings about this "kid," that he decided to accept the challenge.

Joe arrived the following week and immediately began formally surveying the employees. With a schedule that allowed him to be at the company only two days a week, it took another four weeks to gather the information he wanted.

When Joe was ready for a meeting, Alex set aside an entire morning so they could have the proper time to review Joe's findings. Alex had always loved learning, and he was excited by the prospect of expanding his already impressive knowledge about business. He was not prepared for what he heard.

"Al, this is not easy for me to say, but you've got a pretty dysfunctional community here, and you're a major player in that dysfunction."

Alex was shocked and found himself to be unusually defensive. "Me? What are you talking about? I know I've been more than fair, and my employees love me."

"Easy, big fella. I know this isn't going to be easy to hear. To look at what I've found, you're going to have to confront some things that may be new and that you may have even been avoiding. I know you're comfortable with logical and intellectual learning, but this is going to take you into a way of thinking that your academic training hasn't touched. We'll be exploring such issues as control, faith, empowerment, and . . . . . love."

Alex looked at him askance. "Sounds like I'm about to go for a ride on the 'California Woo-Woo'!" They chuckled at Alex's play on the Glen Miller classic.

"You got it, partner, and the train is leaving the station. Are you on board?"

"I guess so, but just go easy with that 'touchy-feely' crap. And, make sure we continue to greet each other with a handshake. I'm not ready for all that huggy-kissy stuff."

"Okay, but let's get back to my findings. People do respect you, but they also fear you."

"Me? I'm a pussycat. I bend over backward to let people slide."

"Al, I know you're a really nice guy, sometimes even too nice. You're the kind who lets things build to the point where you explode. It probably doesn't happen very often, but people around you sense a quick trigger and apprehensively wait for the other shoe to drop. Have you ever been told that before?"

Alex squirmed uncomfortably. This is not how he expected the discussion to go, and he was embarrassed by what he was hearing. "Jane is the only person who's ever said anything like that to me. Sometimes I get frustrated with her when we talk about things like her lateness and messiness. I might raise my voice, but that's as far as it goes . . . usually. I guess there was a time when I lost it and got pretty angry and yelled at her, but that only happened once."

"We'll come back to that later, but what about here at work? I got feedback from folks who said they have either felt devastated being at the other end of your anger or have seen or heard what happens to those who upset you. They see you as very caring, yet very task-oriented and focused on getting the job done. They respect your talent and your ability to see what has to be done and your ability to tell people what they need to do. But they also see you as being very critical when things don't go as you think they should."

Slipping into his take-charge guy mode, Alex sat up straighter and said "Listen, I can't help it if these people are thin-skinned. I don't expect anything more of them than I expect of myself. When there's a job to be done, you just have to do it. And when you screw up, you need to hear about it. What's wrong with that?"

"Al, I'm not here to tell you what's right or wrong. But there are consequences from taking that attitude. I think the lack of trust and fear around this place is a direct result of how conflicts are handled. And it's not just you. Your people feel the same about all the supervisors. Do you know what they call you?"

"No."

"Simon Legree."

Alex sunk into his chair and pensively shared his thoughts with Joe, "I know I'm not very good at dealing with conflicts. It's the same at home with Jane and Peter. I either explode or stuff my feelings. I don't think it's very good for them or our relationship, but I never thought that was relevant in business. And besides, what else is there?" The answer opened up a whole new world for Alex.

Heart Learning

In confronting his tendency to deny problems and maintain his "nice guy" image, Alex threw himself into learning more about the parts of himself that seemed to disappear when faced with difficulties, namely, his compassion and openness to learning. He explored what it would mean to keep his heart open rather than to either emotionally withdraw or to energetically jump into a "fix it mode." He learned about processing differences rather than either immediately giving solutions or ignoring problems.

This focus on relationships led to lots of time being spent talking with Joe about his relationships with Jane and Peter. It was fascinating for him to see how the same dynamics in his business relationships also extended to his family. The issues around control and rebellion, withdrawal and distance, and feelings of resentment and anger that built up around not being heard and appreciated were directly transferable to what was going on at the office.

His personal work led to developing a personal Mission Statement, which he kept on his desk. It read: "I am dedicated to creating a workplace that is emotionally and physically safe and empowers employees by developing their loving abilities as well as their job skills." He also had one for his desk at home which read: "I am dedicated to creating a home that is emotionally and physically safe and empowers family members by developing their loving abilities as well as their intellectual skills."

With his typical response to a challenge, Alex diligently searched for people who modeled both loving behavior and had been successful in the business world. Whether in business or social situations, he found himself bringing almost every conversation around to this subject. He gathered many recommendations for books and tapes of respected business people who were successful in not compromising their caring attitudes and feelings.

One such person was Jim Autry, president of a large division of a Fortune 500 company. Alex devoured Jim's books, being especially touched by *Love and Profit* and *Confessions of an Accidental Businessman*. Alex knew he must meet this man, so one morning he picked up the phone and called Jim. To his surprise, Jim took the call. At the conclusion of a wonderful conversation, they planned to get together in person.

The moment Alex entered Jim's building, he was aware that something was very different. Everyone seemed content and genuinely eager to be of service, but there was something else that he couldn't quite put his finger on. As he climbed the stairs to Jim's office, he thought, "Is it the energy in this place?"

He brought himself up short and thought to himself, "What's with you? Talking about energy. That's weird. You sound like Joe. Sometimes I worry about you. Next thing you know you'll be hugging a tree, or, worse, another guy."

Jim greeted him with a warm smile and much to Alex's relief they shook hands. After exchanging pleasantries, Jim suggested a tour of the plant. As they walked, Alex commented about his sense that something was unusual in the work environment. "I've been trying to put my finger on it." he said. "There seems to be a lack of fear, and . . . I'm not sure. What else is in the air?"

"Joy?" Jim smilingly chimed in.

Alex sighed in recognition, "Yeah, that's it. I've never felt that in a workplace. How do you do that? But before you answer, would you mind if I tape our conversation?"

Jim acknowledged being comfortable with that idea. As they continued walking, Alex started the tape recorder he had brought for just such an opportunity, and Jim shared some of his ideas about management.

[The following ideas are excerpts from an actual conversation that took place between the author and Jim Autry prior to Jim's retirement from Meredith Corporation.]

"I believe that if you create a workplace where people are cared about, all the business objectives will be accomplished. I feel an ethical and moral responsibility to take care of people's money, both the stockholders' and my bosses', so I pay attention to profit. But I don't start out with a goal of creating a certain amount of money.

"I begin with the goal of creating a workplace that is regenerative and facilitates people in establishing satisfying relationships, and doing, most of the time, what they like. I define for myself the aspects of this kind of environment and I write down where people can feel fulfilled by growing personally and spiritually, contributing to the common enterprise, and enjoying the rewards and satisfaction as expressed psychologically, spiritually, physically, and financially of a job well done. I believe this builds a community in the workplace that results in good products, profit, return on investment, and increased shareholder value.

"I want to accomplish all the things the technocrats seek to do, but my focus is entirely different. My primary and overriding goal is to create a caring environment. I have faith that the bottom line will take care of itself. Commitment to the bottom line doesn't mean a damn thing if you can't get good work. Good work comes from employees who care, and people care when they feel cared about.

"You can't cheerlead people into profit. You can only say 'let's be proud of our work and get some sense of enjoyment and meaning from doing it.' When we have created a place where people look forward to their workday, work will exceed expectations, and profit will naturally follow. We don't even have to think about it.

"Business is commerce and commerce is a force. Business is a way of organizing resources in order to do commerce. Technical skills are needed, but once they are gained, business is conceived and revealed through the intellect and imagination of people. It's all people—customers, vendors, investors, and employees.

"People are the transcendent force beyond one of the resources. That's why I don't like the term human resources. I'm not a human resource. I'm a person, and there's a transcendent value to human beings. There's a great middle ground that is the confluence of the caring approach to the people and the intelligent technical approach to the resources. That's the balance I seek. Once you've mastered the technical stuff and understand that the rest is all people, then that balance can be attained."

Their conversation left Alex in an altered state. He had never heard a powerful and successful businessman speak like that. Later than night, as he lay in bed, he thought, "I have so much to learn from him and it's so much more than his ideas. It's where they come from. He's soft and compassionate and yet so powerful. Whether I'm in his presence, or reading his poetry, it feels like a spiritual experience. I want to bring him to our company and have him talk to both our employees and senior management."

He picked up *Confessions of an Accidental Businessman* and opened to page 205 where he read Jim's poem, "On Firing a Salesman":

It is like a little murder.
Taking his life,
his reason for getting on the train,
his lunches at fancy restaurants,
and his meetings in warm and sunny places
where they all gather,
these smiling men,
in sherbet slacks and blue blazers,
and talk about business
but never about prices,
never breaking that law
about the prices they charge.

But what about the prices they pay?
What about gray evenings in the bar car
and smoke-filled clothes and hair
and children already asleep
and wives who say
"You stink"
when they come to bed?
What about the promotions they don't get,
the good accounts they lose
to some kid
because somebody thinks their energy is gone?

What about those times they see in a mirror
or the corner of their eye
some guy at the club shake his head
when they walk through the locker room
the way they shook their heads years ago
at an old duffer
whose handicap had grown along with his age?

And what about this morning,
the summons,
the closed door,
somebody shaved and barbered and shined
fifteen years their junior

> trying to put on a sad face
> and saying he understands?
>
> A murder with no funeral,
> nothing but those quick steps outside the door,
> those set jaws,
> those confident smiles,
> that young disregard for even the thought
> of a salesman's mortality.

Alex closed his eyes and rested the book on his chest. Student and mentor blended together in refreshing sleep.

Alex's return home coincided with Joe being at the company for one of his regularly scheduled visits. Alex excitedly called him into his office. After fifteen minutes of effusively sharing what he had learned from his visit with Jim, he paused and became sad and pensive.

"What's going on?" asked Joe.

"I feel as if I have so far to go to be the way I would like to be. I don't know if I'll ever get there."

"Where's there?" Joe caringly asked.

"Being like Jim."

"Sounds like there's a critical parent in this room, and it's not in my head."

Alex relaxed with a smile. "Yep, I can sure get down on myself."

"How would a loving parent respond right now?"

"I guess he'd assure me that where I am in my life is just fine, and maybe remind me that Jim has been around a lot longer than I have, and probably was not the way he is right now when he was my age. And even if he was, this is my movie and its star is making his way at his own pace, and he's doing pretty damn well. Wow, that feels better. Thanks a lot, Joe."

"Alex, do you realize that I didn't do anything except give you the space to change the channel on the television set in your head from the critical channel to the compassionate channel? There's simultaneous programming going on all the time and all you have to do is change the channel."

"I always forget that, not only with myself, but with others as well. I usually get stuck thinking I'm supposed to be the leader who has the answers and tells people how they're supposed to be, and what they're supposed to do. I think that's why I've avoided engaging with my employees. I'm always afraid that if they come to me with their problems, I'm going to have to solve their problems. Or, if something comes up in a meeting that they need to work on, we'll have to take the time to deal with it."

Joe counseled, "It's so much easier when you know that your responsibility is just to keep your heart open. Like it says in your company value statement, 'Our work is the vehicle for our personal learning.' Your job is just to help them discover their edges and point them in the right direction. You can suggest possible avenues for them to follow, like books, therapy, religion, twelve-step programs, or co-counseling, but it is their responsibility to decide on, and pursue, a course of action. That's all you have to do with your supervisees and all your supervisors have to do with those they supervise."

Alex sat back and sighed, "It seems so easy and yet, sometimes, it's so damn difficult."

Being Your Own Hero, Fulfilling Connections and Possibilities

Alex and Joe diligently worked to develop the personnel procedures and training programs to implement the company's Mission and Values Statement. They were determined to make it more than just pretty-sounding words. Their thinking was consolidated in the following page, which was added to the company personnel manual:

MUTUAL RESPECT AND TRUST

We are committed to creating a work place where everyone is treated in a dignified manner. This important consideration goes beyond our comprehensive sexual harassment and discrimination policy to include any instance where an individual's integrity is violated.

Mutual respect forms the foundation for an environment where a high level of trust exists among management, employees, and our customers. Our effectiveness as a company depends on such trust. A high level of trust will keep us second to none in encouraging employees to be their best and in delivering high quality services to our customers.

To accomplish this we must maintain an openness to learning when diversity issues surface. Diversity occurs anytime people hold differing beliefs or truths. Therefore, it is a natural part of life.

When difficulties result from diversity, we are committed to finding resolutions that respect each person's integrity. This insures that mistakes, failures, unsuccessful attempts at problem solving, or admitting to not knowing will become positive opportunities for learning, rather than negative experiences.

Disrespect enters the work place when individuals are demeaned and their personal boundaries violated, i.e., verbal abuse or sexual harassment. Repeated disrespectful behavior erodes trust. Both managers and supervisors understand that it is disrespectful to allow any behavior that creates an intimidating, hostile, or offensive work environment.

Each person's commitment is needed to mobilize the company policy to make employment at the company an experience that serves to improve trust and, therefore, the quality of life. You are encouraged to talk to your supervisor about any work-related physical or emotional violation. If you are not satisfied, or a safer forum is needed, then speak to an appropriate senior-level manager. If you still seek satisfaction, speak to the President or a designated outside consultant to help resolve any conflicts.

We are committed to being an employer of preference. We want our employees to enjoy working here, and we invite each individual to express any concerns regarding this policy.

To implement the radical changes they envisioned, Alex and Joe knew that teaching the interpersonal skills needed to resolve differences must be part of the company's training program. Alex introduced this idea by relating his own personal experiences at a staff meeting.

He invited his employees to help him by letting him know whenever they felt disrespected in their interactions with him. Although a little uncomfortable at first with his openness, most of his employees were touched by his vulnerability and committed themselves to this new way of being with each other.

In the midst of trying to figure out how to accomplish these new procedures, Alex woke up in the middle of the night with what seemed like a brilliant idea. The next morning he eagerly called a meeting with his supervisors. He proudly introduced the notion of giving equal importance to the accomplishment of tasks and the values of the mission and values statement. He had written the first line of their Mutual Respect and Trust policy on a flip chart, which he unveiled:

**We are committed to creating a workplace
where everyone is treated with dignity.**

"If we are to fulfill our values," he said, "equal importance must be given to completing your projects on time without compromising the integrity of the product or your employees. In this way every task will become a vehicle for modeling our values."

The silence was deafening. It was followed by supervisor after supervisor raising objection after objection. Alex was crestfallen. He called Joe to complain about the lack of creativity and commitment on the part of his supervisors. Joe responded with his typical "every problem is an opportunity" optimism, concluding with, "Well, what's your lesson here? There must be some good reasons they reacted so negatively."

At first Alex felt only irritation with Joe for throwing water on the flame of his quest to rally support for his self-righteousness. And then, his new learning kicked in. He took a deep breath to regain his compassion and proceeded on a fact-finding mission.

He discovered that when he withdrew from the day-to-day operations and left his supervisors in charge, most of them were unprepared. They had been promoted to supervisory positions without adequate selection or training. Their abilities to be big producers were not necessarily the skills needed to lead teams. Whereas when Alex assumed supervisory duties he had pretty good interpersonal skills, most of his salesman did not.

As a result, some of the managers had felt threatened by ideas that were outside their comfort zone. Although they did not openly express their fears, either a lack of interest or overt complaints evidenced the fears. When Alex realized this and understood that these new ideas were not part of the package his supervisors had signed up for when they joined the company, he saw each person in the light of empathy. His entire attitude changed and the energy of compassion was palpable.

Even though his caring could not completely overcome their fears of change, his acceptance and the creation of space for employees to feel heard and considered ameliorated the upheaval, and trust was not diminished. This produced a significantly different result from the environment that typically had accompanied change.

It soon became clear who should remain on the team and who would be better off in an environment that more closely matched what was important to them. Realizing this, some people chose to leave the company, most of them with positive feelings about the company and themselves.

Some did not voluntarily act on the knowledge that this was not the right place for them and had to be fired. But the new procedures detailed a policy that made even this distasteful event palatable. In addition to assistance being given in retraining and relocating, the feelings of those being terminated were compassionately heard. This allowed them to feel respected, even in the face of things not going the way they would have liked.

Upon hiring new employees, Alex instituted a well-defined operational system that radically altered the hiring process. Managers could now clearly communicate the values of this community, so employees were chosen as much for their desire to be part of this unique learning community as for their skills.

When the company values became part of the everyday operation, the kind of trust that transformed their system was established. Greater trust substantially reduced the fear of being treated unfairly and helped free people from their fear of making mistakes. With less protectiveness, people felt more cared about, both by their fellow employees and by management. With this new spirit of cooperation, information that was previously withheld was now more freely shared.

All these changes led to greater creativity and productivity. Employees actually had fun at work, felt supported in the evolution of their souls, and looked forward to coming to work. This became a work place that no one had ever dreamed possible.

When the adversarial atmosphere between management and labor evaporated, differences were resolved amicably. The talks about becoming unionized, which had begun gaining steam before Alex introduced his changes, now fizzled. Naturally, the attitude of the employees got passed on to customers and sales were elegantly reflected on the net profit graph. The ideal of a business that was both profitable and served its employees and the larger community was now being realized.

As Alex continued to "work his program," positive changes happened in all areas of his life and he experienced success and satisfaction in ways he never thought possible. His friendships took on new dimensions as did his family and work relationships. He discovered how to play and have fun. He laughed and cried more easily, and along with that came the physical and emotional intimacy of Fulfilling Connections.

Believe it or not, Alex even became a hugger. He hugged everyone, even those in suits. That was a stretch. Somehow, even though he knew that people in suits probably needed hugs more than anyone, it was difficult for his mind to put hugging and suits together.

When Joe came to visit, Alex could hardly contain himself before throwing his arms around him. But every time their eyes met, Alex still raised a warning eyebrow, cocked his head, and cautioned, "Don't you kiss me!"

The Work Place as a Sanctuary

If learning how to be a more loving person from our relationship with our mate is unusual, and learning how to be a more loving person from our relationship with our children is highly unusual, learning how to be a more loving person from our relationships at work is almost unimaginable. In fact, in my years as a business consultant I learned that the only four-letter word that was never tolerated was the "L" word (unless, of course, you were talking about the love of money).

A work environment contributes substantially to our disconnection when it is not safe to express our feelings and when we are not encouraged to learn from our failures. When people feel their work environment is emotionally unsafe (and this seems to be most people), it means that eight to ten hours a day is spent in a non-nurturing environment.

People tend to think this only happens in high-pressure, profit-driven companies. But businesses reflect the prevailing state of human consciousness throughout our culture, which makes it unsafe to: make mistakes; tell the truth; be confused; not understand; forget; or have opinions, thoughts, or feelings that conflict with those in power. As a result, the environment feels competitive and unsupportive. This kind of work environment can exist in all types of organizations, including educational and political institutions, nonprofit companies, volunteer organizations, and labor unions.

The structure of most organizations puts power in the hands of managers who are not trained to handle interpersonal difficulties with compassion, and its natural by-product, respectful behavior. Inevitable difficulties or disagreements include unmet expectations, broken agreements and promises, and differences of opinion. When faced with difficulties, managers resort to using power for control, the only model they know for dealing with differences. Using power to win or get one's way is disrespectful and creates distrust.

For most people, the only alternative to using power is trying to avoid difficulties by denying them, which also creates distrust and unsafe feelings. For example, the comprehensive leadership-training program of a leading software company does not teach managers how to handle dis-.agreements or upsets. When the program director was asked what people do with their feelings when they are upset, she answered, "They just keep them inside." Walking around with stuffed feelings is a smoldering time bomb that is not nurturing to oneself or to the organization.

Organizations preach the importance of open communication because maximum effectiveness demands it. They often spend large amounts of time and money creating beautiful Mission and Value Statements that idealize this concept. But when everyday interactions leave employees feeling disrespected, everyone knows that the words merely symbolize the hypocrisy in the organization. Using power to control or avoid difficulties ends in the same place—disconnection and distrust.

Using the Power With model with employees occurs when compassion informs our behavior and allows Heart Feelings to guide a process that leads to solutions and Fulfilling Connections. This very unusual approach is illustrated in the following chart that I developed and used when I was employed as a business consultant.

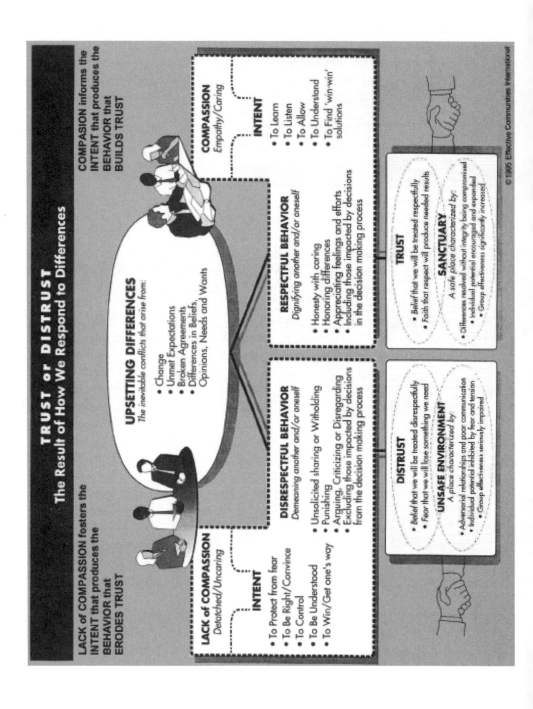

TRUST or DISTRUST
The Result of How We Respond to Differences

LACK of COMPASSION fosters the INTENT that produces the BEHAVIOR that ERODES TRUST

COMPASSION informs the INTENT that produces the BEHAVIOR that BUILDS TRUST

UPSETTING DIFFERENCES
The inevitable conflicts that arise from:
- Change
- Unmet Expectations
- Broken Agreements
- Differences in Beliefs, Opinions, Needs and Wants

COMPASSION
Empathy/Caring

INTENT
- To Learn
- To Listen
- To Allow
- To Understand
- To Find 'win-win' solutions

RESPECTFUL BEHAVIOR
Dignifying another and/or oneself
- Honesty with caring
- Honoring differences
- Appreciating feelings and efforts
- Including those impacted by decisions in the decision making process

TRUST
- Belief that we will be treated respectfully
- Faith that respect will produce needed results

SANCTUARY
A safe place characterized by:
- Differences resolved without integrity being compromised
- Individual potential encouraged and expanded
- Group effectiveness significantly increased

LACK of COMPASSION
Detached/Uncaring

INTENT
- To Protect from fear
- To Be Right/Convince
- To Control
- To Be Understood
- To Win/Get one's way

DISRESPECTFUL BEHAVIOR
Demeaning another and/or oneself
- Unsolicited sharing or Withholding
- Punishing
- Arguing, Criticizing or Disregarding
- Excluding those impacted by decisions from the decision making process

DISTRUST
- Belief that we will be treated disrespectfully
- Fear that we will lose something we need

UNSAFE ENVIRONMENT
A place characterized by:
- Adversarial relationships and poor communication
- Individual potential inhibited by fear and tension
- Group effectiveness seriously impaired

© 1995 Effective Communities International

150

Applying the Trust and Distrust Chart

In the business situation that follows, put yourself in the position of a supervisor or leader. In this way, even if you have not been faced with these situations, you will be learning more about opening your heart in situations that may occur in other areas of your life. For example, in this situation discipline is required. The previous chapter illustrated a discipline situation with a child, but discipline is often necessary with adults as well. Unfortunately, when adults discipline other adults, they usually become parental and treat other adults with the same disrespectful behavior they use with children.

Your secretary is habitually late and it is compromising the efficiency of your office. You have not said anything hoping that things would change. But her irresponsible behavior seems to be getting worse. Disconnection from your compassion (the left side of the chart), allows your resentment to boil over into an irritated outburst accompanied with criticism and penalties. As with most disrespectful responses, you justify your behavior. This time it is justified by the grievousness of her behavior and the right to get your needs met. Just as with a child, muted compassion discounts the feelings of the person at the other end of your hardness.

On the right side of the chart, your discipline is compassionate. You remember that there are always very compelling reasons for behavior, and that knowledge fuels a desire to approach her with a desire to learn what is going on. Keeping your heart open allows you to maintain your caring for her, without losing sight of your own very important needs. Engaging in a Heart Learning process allows both of you to feel heard and respected. The end result is a solution that reflects compassionate discipline.

The Heart Learning process often results in problems being resolved without discipline, but if some kind of discipline is needed it grows out of the process. It will be unique to the situation and the person. Most important, the capacity of each person to be more loving toward themselves and others will be enhanced by the process. Being of service in this way creates Fulfilling Connections.

The following three situations illustrate the difference between a) an environment that erodes trust, and b) one that builds trust.

1. Your work group has been given a new project to complete.

a) You try motivating others by creating a competitive environment with statements such as "As downsizing shrinks the jobs around here only the best and the brightest will be retained. A lack of responsibility will not be tolerated. So, I don't want to hear any bellyaching. If you want a job when this project is completed, you gotta get tough, work smart, and get the job done!"

b) You create a cooperative environment. Hearing each person's perceptions of the task to be completed begins the project and the part each feels he or she can play. You say things like "I am committed to maintaining an environment that will best serve both our employees and the company. When difficulties arise, and I'm sure they will, I want to hear your concerns and suggestions. They will be heard without any reprisals. We will always try our best to meet your needs. I know these are merely words until you test them out, so if you ever come across a situation where anyone in this organization, including myself, has not lived up to this commitment, please let me know."

2. Rumors have begun circulating that a major change in company policy is imminent. If the change happens, you are one of the people who will be affected.

a) On a Friday afternoon a directive concerning the change is passed out as you leave work. From what it says, and you are not exactly sure why and no explanation is given, it looks as though your income will be cut and there is a chance you might be laid off in the future.

b) You are invited to be part of discussions regarding the fiscal dilemma facing the company and the possibility that some employees will have to be laid off. You are encouraged to express your feelings about the effects the change will have and to offer suggestions on how things could be improved at the company.

3. Your boss has been grooming you for advancement in the company. He has invested a great deal in your development, and the two of you have actually become good friends. A person from your hometown contacts you to tell you about a position that has opened up in her company. Your heart is tugged toward the simplicity and quiet of the life you once knew. You decide to take the job.

a) When you tell your boss there is a distinct edge in his voice as he says, "I'm really upset that you would leave me high and dry. I thought I knew you, but I guess I don't. After all we've worked and planned for, I can't believe you would just up and leave. This is a serious breech of trust, and if you follow through on this don't expect to ever work for this company again."

b) With understanding and vulnerability he says, "I'm really disappointed. It's difficult to invest a lot in a relationship and then have it end. A part of me feels that old, familiar feeling of abandonment." With a heartfelt sigh he continues, "Well, I guess this is another opportunity to deal with my stuff. Part of me just wants to convince you to stay. Another part knows that although I'm going to miss you, your happiness is important to me. And I really understand the pull of a simpler life. In fact, I think I'm a little bit envious. I often think of how much I'd love to get out of the rat race. I really want to keep in touch. And if things don't work out, I'd love to see if we can work together again."

Connecting Your Heart to Your Work

Whatever your work, whether as a homemaker or in the business world, try to imagine the following scenario:

> While engaged in your work you feel like it's play rather than work. You feel a great deal of caring from and toward, those around you. You are supported and encouraged to reach new levels of competence in your intellectual, emotional, spiritual, creative, and physical abilities. You are instrumental in assisting others in reaching new levels of competence in their intellectual, emotional, spiritual, creative, and physical abilities. Best of all, you feel that doing your job is congruent with who you really are, and that in doing it you are taking really good care of yourself. Infused with Heart Feelings, you experience many moments of Fulfilling Connections.

It is a sad commentary that in this most vital area of our lives, most people experience few moments of Fulfilling Connection. When hearts open at work we use our unique talents to create something of value, for example, material goods, works of art, challenging and meaningful ideas, or services, such as giving comfort to ourselves and others. When our hearts are connected to what we are doing, we are creating a work place that is a sanctuary.

Since productivity seems to be a natural instinct in nondomesticated animals, it is logical to assume that humans as well have a natural drive toward being productive. However, our capacity for more complex development than other life forms makes the task of knowing how to fulfill ourselves in our work quite challenging.

Discovering and developing our unique talents is one of the most important pursuits we can undertake. A major part of this process depends on nurturing Heart Feelings. These are the feelings that will lead us to the activities that feel right inside, leave us feeling good about ourselves, and give meaning to our lives.

The following account of the beginning of my search for a fulfilling career illustrates the difference between work that connects to Heart Feelings and what happened when I was disconnected from them.

Even though I had dutifully fulfilled the requirements of my college education, I found little of value in it, and upon graduation from college was still clueless about what I wanted to do when I grew up. Had I been connected to my compassion, the first job I had out of college would have probably been satisfying.

I was hired as a personnel specialist at Litton Industries. That corporation, which was to become an international giant, was just a fledgling company at the time. There were plenty of opportunities to be of service, but I wasn't interested. At that time, I had no idea that I was a very compassionate, highly sensitive, very emotional person with a strong desire to be of service to others. Four highly undistinguished years later, I left my personnel career to begin training as a stockbroker.

After learning the technical aspects of the brokerage business, I was pronounced ready to be a salesman. Talk about a fish out of water! Without a strong connection to my internal compass, I had no idea that a business in which the only thing of importance seemed to be making money had little to offer me. Not surprisingly I floundered, while losing money for my family and friends (to whom else do you begin selling stocks?). Finally, the inevitable day arrived when, by mutual consent, the company and I decided to part ways.

Three other equally disconnected attempts to find a career followed and all ended in disaster. At twenty-seven and still drifting, I met Margie. Two months into our relationship she said, "Have you ever been happy doing anything at which you think you could make a living?"

"The only thing I've ever enjoyed doing was coaching the kids at the YMCA," I replied.

"Well, what about teaching?" she said.

"Are you kidding?" I shot back. "Teachers don't make enough money for a decent living!"

I never expected the next words I heard. To this day, they are the most important words anyone has ever said to me: "I don't think that we need much money to be happy," she said, "but I know that we don't have a chance of being happy if you're not fulfilled in your work. If you want to go into teaching, I'm behind you all the way."

I spent the next year getting my teaching credential and the rest of my life reflects a complete reversal from my first twenty-seven years. The moment I stepped into the classroom I felt, for the first time, at home.

I subsequently learned that the reason I loved teaching and was an excellent teacher was that teaching allowed me to express who I really was inside and out. There, in my tiny classroom, I could connect to the compassionate, highly sensitive person within and make a significant difference in the lives of my students. I had the freedom to be humorous, creative, and full of feeling. The more fully I developed these aspects of my soul, the more successful I became and the more I felt like my own hero.

The fact that each of us has unique talents is an important factor in fulfilling our productivity drive. Those with greater mechanical abilities tend to be drawn toward engineering. Logical thinkers usually gravitate toward computers, science, business, or accounting. Those who have a facility for dealing with people seek positions in sales or supervision. Those with greater sensitivity and empathy choose occupations in which being of service is of primary importance, such as social work, homemaking, teaching, and medicine.

Merely finding our niche in the areas where we are most comfortable does not seem to be all that we need to satisfy us. Since satisfying productivity occurs when unique talents combine with Heart Feelings, any task can be filled with Fulfilling Connections.

When connected to one's heart, anyone, from housewives and mothers to factory workers and salespeople, can experience more fulfillment and meaning from whatever they are doing. This is consistent with the Buddhist idea that anything can be a meditation, whether folding laundry, raising children, or running a corporation.

Many of the things people do for a living can only be done when disconnected from Heart Feelings. For example, compassion is definitely dormant in the people who work in industries that befoul our environment or create products that negatively affect our health and well-being, such as individuals who work in the tobacco industry.

But even in jobs that provide a service such as teaching, medicine, and law, satisfaction cannot be found when we are disconnected from Heart Feelings. This occurs when, for example:

- Teachers become so preoccupied with teaching subject matter that they lose touch with the needs of their students
- Physicians enter the field of medicine without the motivation to be of service, which was the primary incentive for people going into medicine fifty years ago
- Lawyers lose sight of their charge to engage in a search for the truth in favor of the creation of billable hours

In each of the above situations, the opportunity to gain satisfaction and meaning from serving oneself and others has succumbed to a different master, such as duty, money, winning, or power.

Although it is possible to use Heart Feelings in most jobs, doing so is often frowned upon within most established institutions. Using your Heart Feelings where you work requires both a great deal of courage and the security in knowing that you have the right to employ them. You have only to read or see movies about people who went against tremendous odds in their profession to utilize their Heart Feelings to get a glimpse into why you may not be using yours.

In addition to the prohibitions within institutions, our internal critic is ever vigilant on its job of keeping us from developing and using our Heart Feelings. For example, the task of parenting, one of the most significant jobs we ever undertake, has the incredible potential to be one of the most satisfying experiences of our lives, but too often it is not. We could be experiencing many moments of Fulfilling Connection by nurturing the Heart Feelings of our children. There is no boss threatening to fire us if we do not spend time with our children connected to our Heart Feelings in play, touch, or learning, yet the many opportunities to do so are so often missed.

To find the satisfaction from parenting that can only come from Fulfilling Connections means encouraging our children's ability to play by playing with them; to touch by touching and being touched by them; to learn about themselves by providing an emotionally safe environment in which to express themselves; and learning how to more fully develop our abilities to be more nurturing to ourselves and our children. When we use our Heart Feelings, parenting is profoundly satisfying work.

Can you imagine creating more Fulfilling Connections in your work by using your Heart Feelings to produce something of value? It might mean producing a consumer product that will benefit others; being touched by the lives of your coworkers and giving comfort to them; or doing a business report that reflects your caring and compassion.

A couple of questions that might help you focus your thinking about finding greater fulfillment in your work are:

1. What prevents me from keeping my heart open and being touched by, and playful with, my clients, students, customers, employees, or family members? Is it just the fear of disapproval from others, or is it that omnipresent "infernal" critic that keeps me from letting go and enjoying these parts of myself?
2. What keeps me from nurturing these abilities in others and myself in the course of fulfilling my job obligations?

The answers to questions like these point you in the direction of learning to connect your heart to whatever you are doing. Whenever Heart Feelings are present, work does not fit the definition of work that you may be carrying around in your head. It is not something you do just for the money you earn. In fact, if you had all the money you desired you would be doing the same thing (perhaps, not so much of it, however). It gives you pleasure and is fulfilling while it adds to your self-esteem and sense of being your own hero. It is a possible dream. It requires finding your heart and bringing it into your work.

Chapter Eight

Evaluating Relationships

When reaching for something new, the way one goes about it greatly influences the outcome.

—Joel Kramer & Diana Alstad,
The Guru Papers: Masks of Authoritarian Power

Relationships are an integral part of our journey toward increased moments of Fulfilling Connection and feeling like our own heroes. We are always in relationship with ideas, the organizations and practitioners that dispense those ideas, other people, and, most important, with ourselves. Relationships illuminate our direction by telling us what we are looking for—even when we are not consciously aware of what that may be.

For example, if we are seeking answers from outside ourselves, we will be attracted to individuals, or perhaps programs, that promise answers. Conversely, if we deeply desire the wisdom that facilitates becoming our own heroes, we will be attracted to people and programs that provide us with the ability to discover our own truths. Simply put, what we bring to the table determines the kind of meal we will be served. There is no right or wrong diet, but there certainly are very different menus.

Some of the possible relationships on our paths were illustrated in each of the six preceding stories. For example, I was helped by a psychotherapist, a men's group, and a best friend; Andrea by a teacher and faith community; Alex by a consultant; Shawna by a community resource; George by a friend, books, films, and journal writing; and Bill and Marie by a leaderless self-help group.

The people and ideas illustrated in this chapter are meant to help answer the questions "Whom do I turn to for help?" and "How do I evaluate the help that I'm getting?" It will help you recognize the often subtle ideas that exist in every person or philosophy that disconnect you from your heart and impede your journey.

No person or path is perfect. Even philosophies based on the teaching of highly enlightened people are interpreted and institutionalized by teachers who are acculturated with blind spots. For example, the scholarly and well-meaning people who interpret Jesus' teachings are not as highly evolved as Jesus was and, as a result, the Catholic religion has become infiltrated with Disconnecting Beliefs. Kevin Smith illuminated this in his controversial film *Dogma*. Many people criticized the film as being anti-Catholic, but Smith maintains that he is very religious and observant to the essence of his faith, and that the film merely exposes the dogmatic thinking that is inconsistent with Jesus' message.

Dogmatic thinking that disconnects us from our hearts is certainly not the exclusive province of Catholicism. The same process of losing the message of total acceptance and love that was the essence of the teaching of enlightened masters has affected every institutionalized discipline. It is evidenced in this orthodox Jewish prayer: "Blessed art thou, O Lord, who hast not made me a woman." It is also a part of Buddhism, in this idea: "You have to be born a man to attain enlightenment." With heightened awareness, you will be able to dismiss those notions that create Disconnecting Beliefs while continuing on your current path; or, you may discover that it is appropriate to find a new path.

Since Disconnecting Beliefs, especially those related to power, exist in all people, leaders often do not facilitate becoming your own hero and thus fail to empower their constituents. That includes religious leaders, politicians, social reformers, business icons, teachers, physician-healers and parents. Those leaders who need to be in control covet the power that is gained from keeping people dependent. Empowering constituents is antithetical to a need for control because people who have a strong connection to their Heart Feelings have an inner knowing that would never allow giving away personal power and becoming dependent on an authority outside of themselves.

To evaluate the ideas you are being taught, and to assess whether your leadership is facilitating or frustrating becoming your own hero, the following question can be used as a screen through which to filter the information you are receiving.

Are the ideas I am receiving, and the people who are giving me guidance, helping me develop the wisdom that is moving me:

- toward feeling like my own hero by encouraging Heart Feelings and Fulfilling Connections with myself and others with whom I am involved
- away from being self-righteous, judgmental, a victim, manipulating others; dependent on substances, other people, the teacher or group; and making gaining power through winning or getting my way a primary goal?

If the above is happening, the following should be resulting:

1. By embracing more of the thoughts, feelings, and actions in yourself and others, your self-worth and self-trust is increasing.
2. By helping you find your own answers, rather than being told what you should do, what is healthy, and what is right, your self-esteem is increasing.
3. Both/And rather than Either/Or thinking is being encouraged.
4. You are becoming less sure and more secure.
5. Others are more comfortable around you, and you are more comfortable with yourself and by yourself.
6. You are being helped to respect and feel loving toward yourself, rather than feeling guilty, wrong, or as though you are not enough.
7. You are being helped to integrate into your viewpoint a larger picture of life by seeing your connectedness to other people, the earth, the universe, and to an intelligence that lies beyond your conscious mind.
8. You are being encouraged to affiliate yourself with and to find healing from many sources, rather than believing that there is only one way.
9. You are being helped to establish respectful and loving relationships with others both within and outside your group, rather than being encouraged to convert others to your way of thinking and/or enrolling them in a particular philosophy.
10. Life is becoming more meaningful and you are feeling more peaceful, content, and less tense.

As stated at the beginning of this chapter, "No path is perfect." Within almost every discipline or person, there are ideas and interactions that are both healing and wounding. By becoming more adept at embracing your heart and rejecting the instruments that wound, you will take better care of yourself and will be better able to create more Fulfilling Connections. The remainder of this chapter investigates relationships from that perspective. The question addressed is "What ideas and interactions empower natural abilities with Heart Feelings and heal the wounds that lead to giving away your power?"

Since all healing relationships are therapeutic, psychotherapy is presented first because the ideas discussed are integral to every relationship. (Note: To resolve the omnipresent dilemma of how to respectfully use pronouns, "he" and "she" will be used in alternate paragraphs.)

Psychotherapy

The following ideas about psychotherapy are narrowly focused only on those times when you desire an empowering therapeutic relationship that facilitates Fulfilling Connections and becoming your own hero. Sometimes you may not want this. You may want someone to tell you what to do or someone to support your way of seeing things. Other times, you may just want relief for the symptoms that may be resulting from deeper issues. There is no right or wrong way to want psychotherapy.

Not every type of psychotherapy is appropriate for the journey toward becoming your own hero. Curing phobias or biochemical imbalances requires a specific kind of treatment quite different from one that heals the wounds of disconnection. That kind of healing calls for a philosophy that honors the integrity of your struggle to find meaning and purpose. Humanistic, Jungian, and Transpersonal schools of psychology meet this criterion. But just because a tradition honors a philosophy does not mean that its practitioners facilitate it.

Therapeutic relationships are not those commonly thought of by phrases like "Don't therapize me!" or "I hate it when you psychoanalyze me!" or "Cut out that psychobabble!" Healing relationships embody the definition of a therapist in the sense of the Greek word from which therapy is derived, "therapon" which means "comrades in a common struggle." Becoming your own hero is facilitated in a therapeutic relationship that creates a safe place for you to learn. In such places you can expose what you believe are the darkest parts of yourself with relative assurance that you will be treated respectfully.

Becoming your own hero is promoted when a therapist, by focusing on your tendency to judge and distrust yourself, helps you to embrace all of yourself. When a therapist takes sides, judges, has an agenda for how you should "be," or tells you what to do, she is trying to change you.

Communicating that you need to change is not accepting you as you are. It is, therefore, not respectful, becoming your own hero is frustrated, and you are disempowered. At times, it may be appropriate for the therapist to make suggestions or to be a teacher, but this must be engaged in very judiciously. Looking to others to tell you what to do and telling others what to do are both habit forming.

Becoming your own hero is facilitated when a therapist does not participate in attempts to get him to take responsibility for you. His response to you wanting him to solve your problem might be as my therapist responded when I asked him, "What do you think I should do?" He just sympathetically said, "I wish I could give you some simple ideas that would make your pain immediately disappear, but I can't. I take back what I just said. Even if I could wave a magic wand I wouldn't. I don't believe advice is what you need. I want to help you discover how to trust your inner knowing."

When you ask your therapist to tell you what is best for you, she helps you understand why looking to others for answers is demeaning, and helps you uncover the beliefs that drive that tendency. Should she succumb to the temptation of telling you what to do (and since she is human she probably will at times), when she realizes that she has become caught in her Disconnecting Beliefs, she will, with humility, discuss what she did and its consequences.

A therapist may dazzle you with his ability to interpret dreams, analyze situations, give solutions, theorize about why you are feeling or thinking as you are, or the childhood that created your thoughts and feelings. This may impress you, but it is of little, if any, value in helping you embrace and believe in yourself, and thus move out of dependency and into self-trust. Rather, it encourages dependency on him for analysis and answers.

Compassionate listening facilitates becoming your own hero. When a therapist "gets with you," it promotes feeling understood, cared about, and respected. It communicates that the therapist believes in you. This helps you believe in yourself. It is like coming up from a suffocating sea of communications, into a breath of fresh air.

Labeling behavior frustrates becoming your own hero because labels put you into boxes of right and wrong behavior. They place you into neat, psychological categories such as neurotic, bi-polar, co-dependent, obsessive compulsive, narcissistic, dependent, or addictive. Saying "You are [fill in the blank]" is like being branded with a universal condemnation. Applying a label does not leave you feeling understood, respected, or knowing that there are very important reasons for your behavior, and it is not helpful in overcoming those reasons.

Becoming your own hero is facilitated when a therapist remains objective, walking the fine line of being both neutral and supportive. She does not jump into your stories and believe them either to be true or not true. She knows that stories are true from your perspective, but that doesn't mean they actually happened or happened in the way you are relating them.

To believe a story that is not true supports delusional thinking, being a victim, and blaming others. For example, should a repressed memory surface, a therapist can support your reality as reported without either believing or disbelieving it. It is not important to determine whether an event actually happened. Becoming your own hero is facilitated by the therapist helping you understand your reality, affirming the very good reasons you have for creating it, understanding both the negative and positive consequences that are attached to every decision, and giving support should you decide to confront whatever demons are keeping you locked in.

Becoming your own hero is facilitated by the belief that we all struggle and strive toward being more consistent in our loving. This knowledge is not communicated when a therapist remains removed and aloof. It is communicated through his willingness to be transparent and communicate his own humanness. He does this by sharing times when he feels stuck and unsure, or when his heart closes, and what he feels and does when he experiences those conditions. It is an attitude that communicates that you are not alone or hopeless and that no one is loving all the time. It communicates that we are truly comrades in a common struggle.

Becoming your own hero is facilitated when a therapist helps you realize that "talking therapy" is only helpful up to the point of getting you ready to test out your fears. Jerry's story illustrates this idea.

Jerry was 100 pounds overweight when he entered therapy. He was lonely and unhappy and wanted help losing weight. In the first few sessions he talked about his ongoing battle with losing weight, beginning in junior high school. He had been in therapy previously and was very conversant with all the reasons for his obesity, including his controlling mother, abusive older sister, and his fears of intimacy.

When Jerry related the one time he had shed his extra baggage of pounds, I got a glimpse into the direction we needed to go. Jerry had entered a hospital program that required rigid monitoring. In that environment he successfully reached his goal of 180 pounds and was released with honors. He bought a whole new wardrobe and felt great showing off his svelte new body. Women responded to him positively for the first time in his life. A few indicated that they wanted to go out with him. He had been at his ideal weight for only three months when he started to gain the weight back. Within another two months he was back to 280 pounds.

Jerry clearly remembered the terror he felt about the thought of dating and possibly being intimate with a woman. Although a major fear was being sexually inadequate, an even deeper terror lay in his fear that if he was "in love" he would do anything to not lose that relationship, including giving up himself. Even though it was painful being alone, it was a lot safer than having to confront those demons.

I told him that we could talk theoretically forever about his weight and his fears of being involved, but that until he lost the weight it was just talk. I told him, "When you lose the weight and are up against your fears, you will probably need someone to help you deal with them. I would love to be that person."

After five years Jerry called to say he was ready to begin this journey with me. It was an exciting, terrifying, and productive experience.

In group therapy, becoming your own hero is facilitated when members understand Fulfilling Connections and Heart Feelings. Group work is very exciting and empowering when participants are dedicated to Heart Learning about themselves, assisting others in Heart Learning about themselves, and creating a safe environment for that learning to occur.

At times, members have the opportunity to become leaders and share their observations about when Fulfilling Connections are being facilitated or frustrated. At those times, the learning comes from what is going on in the room. Instead of a person bringing in an outside situation and receiving direction from the therapist, each person is involved in the moment, in a dynamic process of learning about how they feel and respond, and what blocks their openness. In a safe environment, real life situations are used as practice for the real-life situations that are waiting outside of the therapy room.

Becoming your own hero is facilitated when the therapist makes it clear that formal therapy is not long term. It is geared to help develop the resources, including supportive relationships, for continuing to expand your Heart Feelings. Returning to therapy may occasionally be needed when you get stuck or need a tune up. It is in learning to use the resources around you to overcome the challenges of life that you build confidence in your ability to create your own sense of well-being.

Personal Growth Workshops and Seminars

Personal growth workshops can be of exceptional value in learning specific skills or ideas. However, depending on the beliefs that are being taught and how they are taught, they also contain the potential for frustrating becoming your own hero. In the hands of a skilled teacher, it is often very difficult to separate fact from fiction. Charismatic teachers can brainwash you and pick your pocket at the same time. Everything depends on the intent of the teachers and the organizations behind them.

Becoming your own hero is frustrated when the teacher or organization is intent on hooking you into a certain belief system or making you dependent on the teacher or organization. This may be consciously planned into how the material is presented, or it may be unintentional. In either case, the result is the same.

The following account was told to me by Charlie Bloom, one of my dearest friends. Charlie has led personal growth workshops for twenty-five years. He entered the seminar world when he went to work for a nationally known training company in the late 70s. It was here he learned how to be in front of a room of people and effectively implant certain predetermined messages.

I met Charlie at a weekend conference in Lake Arrowhead, California, about thirteen years ago. We felt an immediate connection and very quickly were sharing our most intimate thoughts. He was emerging from a yearlong depression that accompanied separating from the company for which he had worked for the past six years.

As we strolled along a spectacular trail in the San Bernardino Mountains, he opened up. "One of the hardest things for me was coming to grips with what I had been doing in the training room that was disempowering for people. It was so subtle that I was not even aware it. Now that I'm aware of it, it doesn't seem so subtle; but at the time I never realized the effect what I was taught to do was having on people."

"Like what?" I asked.

"Well, let's begin at the beginning. When I first took the training as a student, I was deeply moved by the dramatic changes I observed in others and myself. I had some concerns with the trainer's tactics of control and influence. I asked the trainer about this and was assured that such tactics were necessary to break down people's resistance. Then he threw me the zinger: 'How long have you had this issue with authority?'

"I later learned that that's the way it was in the training. Any concern, question, or problem that someone had with the trainer, or the training itself, was treated as if it was an example of the individual's resistance. It was used to explain why the student's life wasn't working. The message that one's life wasn't working served to more effectively control the student by defining him as being in an inferior position relative to the trainer.

"The trainer was presented as the only one in the room whose life was really working. Everything we did and said was deliberately scripted to promote this impression. The way we dressed, wore our hair, and talked about our lives was cultivated to create an appearance of success and power.

"I was taught how to develop an image of unquestionable authority. My mentor continually reminded me that what matters is not what you know, but in creating the illusion of certainty. That meant speaking with authority, whether you knew what you were talking about or not.

"The seminar stressed empowering students to take charge of their lives. But what went on was designed to have the opposite effect. We were intent on getting them to idolize their trainer, thus giving over their power to someone who was omnipotent and omniscient. In this way, we infantalized them. When I realized this I was heartbroken."

At this point Charlie had a hard time choking back his tears. We walked silently for a while before he spoke again. "The more I realized, and there's a lot that I haven't even told you yet, the more unhappy I became, until I finally had to quit. This past year I've spent remembering, feeling tremendous sadness, and contemplating how, if I ever decide to get up in front of a group of people again, I would do it differently."

Luckily for all those people who have taken Charlie's workshops, he did return to the training room. In fact he and his wife Linda have developed a very successful business, The Empowerment Network, which provides personal growth seminars, including men's and women's retreats. That name is very significant to Charlie because he is dedicated to teaching only in ways that empower students.

During our friendship, I have both cofacilitated and taken workshops from Charlie. I have learned a great deal from him about what it means to create a safe and healing environment by never denying the perceptions and feelings of students. He demonstrates the transformative power of being an open and loving teacher who can laugh, cry and share his own struggles without losing an ounce of credibility.

Linda and Charlie have not built an organization that shows megagrowth. They do not live on a large private estate or drive flashy cars. They are, however, very successful and happy in all areas of their lives. Their marriage, on the verge of divorce fifteen years ago, has not only survived, but has been strengthened. Their kids have enjoyed the benefits of a more loving and present father. Charlie and Linda are writing a book about what they have learned whose title perfectly captures what their lives and teachings are all about: *Stronger in All the Broken Places*.

Even when it is not consciously planned into a workshop, being in the presence of an authority immediately puts the student in a one-down position. Fulfilling Connections are facilitated by how this situation is handled. When teachers humbly put out ideas as *their* truths, not as *the* truths, and maintain an attitude of humility and openness when questions and disagreements arise, students are respected and their self-esteem is nurtured.

Religious and Spiritual Disciplines

It is hard to imagine a formalized religion or spiritual movement holding their beliefs lightly. Typically, such disciplines are based on the teachings of an "enlightened" authority, sometimes God himself, that purport to be "the truth." These ideas are detailed in a book that is to be continually contemplated, if not memorized. Institutional movements thrive on attracting devotees who want an infallible source to reveal the information that will make everything turn out all right.

There is no doubt that putting out an idea as *a* truth does not carry the magnetism of beliefs that are put out as *the* truth. However, the important criteria for facilitating becoming your own hero of holding beliefs lightly, cannot be met when there is only one truth.

Becoming your own hero is facilitated when spiritual teachings and teachers support your ability to discover meaning and truth for yourself. This was much more commonplace in the past. Modern inventions from the printing press to television serve our mania for homogenizing differences and sacrificing individual thinking to "authoritative" analysis. Consider that before the printing press, scriptures were read at public gatherings and discussed in small groups for clarity and finding meaning and truth for oneself. The invention of the printing press not only allowed mass distribution, but also for including interpretations that were to be learned and accepted on faith.

Traditional religions are easy targets for illustrating authoritarian-based ideas that separate people from their Heart Feelings and others. Yet, even within tightly scripted disciplines, there are practitioners who transcend many of the separating doctrines and present ideas that help unite us internally and externally.

Such individuals exist in every community. Cecil Williams, a Methodist minister at Glide Memorial Church in San Francisco, California, is one such person. Cecil is unique, and his church is not your stereotypically religious enclave. On any Sunday, Fulfilling Connections can be experienced with people of every imaginable racial, economic, political, and sexual orientation. During the week, programs go on that embrace every area of community difficulties, from addiction and domestic abuse to homelessness and discrimination. It is a church that walks the talk of empowering individuals and creating unity out of diversity.

Outside mainstream disciplines are persuasions that claim to offer alternative ways of embracing spirituality without the dogma of traditional religions, but sometimes miss that mark. *A Course in Miracles* is an example of how even "New Age" philosophies can be authoritarian and thus frustrate becoming your own hero. I chose to exemplify this idea with *A Course in Miracles* because, even though it is a philosophy with a basically positive message, and one from which I personally have gained great value, it still contains some subtle assumptions that perpetuate disconnection.

A Course in Miracles was written by a woman who purportedly channeled a voice that identified itself as the spirit of Jesus Christ. Joel Kramer and Diana Alstad in *The Guru Papers* describe the problems inherent in this approach:

"The Course is but another revealed (by an unchallengeable authority) renunciate ideology that separates the spiritual from the mundane, the pure from the impure, the selfless from the self-centered. It says listen to your own voice, but programs what your voice will say by taking away the validity of experience, reason, thoughts, and disapproved of emotions. Like gurus, it then fills the vacuum it creates with its own renunciate worldview offering the same old coin of eternal bliss. Nothing could be more authoritarian, for who could argue against a disembodied spirit with the credentials of a traditional God? If one were to say (as we do) that one's inner voice says something quite different, then what?"

There is no doubt that *A Course in Miracles*, as with almost every religious and spiritual discipline and teacher, contains many wonderful and supportive ideas. However, being given "truths" without the caveat that they are merely chosen beliefs, or not being allowed to discover what is true for one's self, creates dependency, encourages a false righteousness, and ultimately blocks becoming your own hero.

Since many disciplines and spiritual teachers participate in truth selling rather than truth telling, it is up to you to gain the strength to see past their limitations, gather up the best they offer, reject what offends your self-trust, and seek support from like-minded spiritual seekers.

To facilitate becoming your own hero, perhaps the most important question through which to filter your experiences with religious/spiritual disciplines is "Does the discipline address my desire to rely on authorities and does it help me overcome this tendency?" In *A Path with Heart*, Jack Kornfield poses some questions with which to evaluate a spiritual community:

- Are you asked to violate your own sense of ethical conduct or integrity?
- Is there a dual standard for the community versus the guru and a few people around him?
- Are there secrets, rumors of difficulty?
- Do key members misuse sexuality, money, or power?
- Is there something powerful going on that may not really be loving?
- Is there a sense of intolerance?
- Is the community based on sectarianism or separation or does it have a fundamentalist quality to it?
- Am I becoming more isolated, dependent, obnoxious, lost, or addicted?
- Is there a greater capacity to know what is true for myself, to be compassionate and tolerant?

Kornfield also gives a description of a spiritually mature person, which I believe to be a wonderful standard to use in evaluating your spiritual evolution:

"The spiritually mature person has learned the great arts of staying present and letting go. Their flexibility understands that there is not just one way to practice or one fine spiritual tradition, but there are many ways. They understand that spiritual life is not about adopting any one particular philosophy or set of beliefs or teachings, that it is not a cause for taking a stand in opposition to someone else or something else. It is an easiness of heart that understands that all of the spiritual vehicles are rafts to cross the stream to freedom."

Self-Help Support Groups

Self-help support groups can often be valuable in helping you through difficulties. Those that facilitate becoming your own hero, foster self-trust, and thus do not create dependency on the group itself. In addition, they expand your opportunity to become your own hero by helping you see that all of us are as basically loving and struggling with our woundedness, rather than presenting ideas that disconnect one group from other groups.

For example, men's and women's support groups present wonderful opportunities to create a safe place for people of the same gender to express themselves. When these groups provide a place to gain the strength to recover alienated parts of yourself, they are invaluable in facilitating becoming your own hero. When they foster beliefs that the other gender is bad and responsible for your problems, they frustrate becoming your own hero.

When groups separate into camps of victims wounded by the other side, they become blind to the real enemy—the beliefs that have disconnected us from our Heart Feelings—and miss the opportunity to engage in self-healing. Empowering self-healing comes from overcoming the beliefs that allow us to tolerate wounding behavior and gain the strength to become an active participant in healing the culture of beliefs that perpetuate such wounding.

Leaderless groups do not suffer the problems associated with an authoritarian leader, but unless they operate from guidelines that promote becoming your own hero, they often do not grapple with Disconnecting Beliefs. The twelve-step programs are such an example.

Twelve-step programs are very effective in keeping people free from their drug of choice. They do not, however, address disconnection from Heart Feelings. Without that healing, their effectiveness is limited. Addictive personalities can transfer their addictions to substances that may be less overtly destructive, but unless the disconnection from their Heart Feelings is in the process of being resolved, the fears of loss and the concurrent need to control will still dominate their lives.

The following is a true story, exemplifying the problem of stopping one addiction without addressing the source of the addiction. Alfred, who was known to the author, is now deceased. Out of respect for his memory, I have used a psuedonym.

After alcohol contributed heavily to destroying both a very successful career and his marriage, Alfred joined Alcoholics Anonymous and was saved. He devoted himself to "working the program" and pulling himself out of the gutter. He discovered God and, wanting to bring this gift (God/AA) to others, became trained as a minister.

His substantial charisma and business acumen combined to create tremendous success. He based the teachings of his church on a blend of AA and New Age ideas that taught how positive thinking could create great abundance. This combination drew not only recovering addicts, but also many people who believed they could find the answers to their questions of having more control over their future.

The church prospered. Since everything was done first class, their need for more and more capital to finance their growth grew exponentially. Beautiful buildings were constructed and furnished. Everyone dressed to the "nines," showing the symbols of the wealth they were accumulating. Finely tailored suits, expensive jewelry, and furs were on display at every Sunday service and church event. Although Alfred and his parishioners talked the talk of love, a cancer was growing. The many instances where he and others did not practice love were ignored.

Upon Alfred's sudden death, the congregation was thrown into turmoil. The first shock was finding out that there were millions of dollars unaccounted for and that, as a result, the church was heavily in debt. Closer scrutiny discovered mismanagement that had paid off handsomely for Alfred.

Then what started as a trickle soon became a flood of young women coming forward to tell their stories of being seduced sexually by Alfred. And, of course, there were the many people who either consciously or unconsciously contributed to the veil of silence around both of these indiscretions. This was very disturbing for those who confronted their responsibility in allowing themselves to be led into moral and financial bankruptcy.

One of the morals of the story is how susceptible we all are to addiction and denial. Although Alfred never drank alcohol, he still got drunk on sex and power. Just because we successfully stop one of our addictions does not mean we have confronted the issues that keep us stuck in the grip of the problems created by disconnecting from our self-love and giving up control of our lives to authoritarian powers.

Friends

One person helping another to facilitate becoming his or her own hero creates a special friendship. When Joe told Alex that his company was a dysfunctional community, and that he was a major player in it, Joe became more than a business consultant; he was a friend facilitating Alex becoming his own hero.

Friends who facilitate becoming your own hero:

- Are honest, in a respectful way, with you
- See through your defenses and care enough to give you compassionate feedback, serving you by tapping you on the shoulder when you become defensive and gently saying, "Seems as if you've lost your heart connection"
- Offer you a sounding board upon which to clarify your ideas when you get stuck
- Comfort you, literally and figuratively holding you as you feel your pain in preparation for beginning your intellectual explorations and learning
- Help you lighten up when you've lost your compassion and/or feel overwhelmed or judgmental toward yourself
- Know both the outgoing, loving side of you as well as your shadow side and still value you
- Offer you information when you want it, but don't push those ideas
- Allow you to do all the above with them

When you are with friends who facilitate becoming your own hero you are:

- Free to be yourself and not have to put on a face
- Heard
- Comfortable and safe in knowing that they don't want to control you or have an agenda as to how you should be
- Open to discuss anything and stimulated by those discussions

Relationships that frustrate becoming your own hero occur when you are not supported in opening your heart, when your beliefs are not challenged, and when you are not being helped to take personal responsibility. This occurs from interactions that do not encourage you to stay connected to your Heart Feelings. For example, being given advice that keeps your heart closed by blaming others and feeling like a victim alienates you from your Heart Feelings and alienates you as well from others.

Friendships like this are similar to relationships with gurus who want to keep you tied to them. When a person wants not only to be your best friend, but your only friend, he or she encourages thoughts and feelings that foster exclusivity and lead you to being more and more cloistered and alienated from other friends and even from your own family.

There are many ways to extol the virtues and value of friendships that facilitate becoming your own hero. Finding a person who really cares about you and has your best interests at heart is a wonderful gift. Having a relationship with someone who listens and supports you is a blessing. One of the distinguishing characteristics of falling in love lies in believing that you have found such a person.

Wanting a relationship that facilitates becoming your own hero is a powerful and compelling reason for being with a friend. It usually requires discussions that define your intentions and theirs. Explicitly stating your desire, and asking for the kind of feedback that facilitates it, gives friends permission to confront you when they are aware of things that may have slipped through the cracks of your consciousness.

Friendships that facilitate becoming your own hero will hold a special place in your heart. By creating a place where you feel safe to share your thoughts and feelings in ways that open up unexplored territories, it is therapeutic. It is a challenging and exciting adventure and you feel grateful for having this person in your life.

Formal Education

The education system typically provides little help in facilitating becoming your own hero. In general, formal education is designed to push factual information and rote learning, to pass on established thinking, and foster conformity. It does not value helping students become their own heroes.

Parker Palmer, in *To Know as We Are Known,* describes the disconnection in our educational system in the following way:

"From our [educated people] platform we observe and analyze and assess, but we do not go into the arena—for that is how we have been taught to know. This means that virtues like compassion, the capacity to "feel with" another, are "educated away." In their place arises clinical detachment; counselors and physicians are trained not to get involved with their clients, journalists with their stories, lawyers with their cases. Involvement has its problems, but is detachment the solution?"

My personal experience in teacher education vividly illustrates what Palmer is talking about. In my last teacher education class before being sent out to be a student teacher, the coup de grace warning of my professor was "Don't ever become personally involved in the lives of your students." He went on to justify his statement with a long detailed story about the devastation experienced by a good friend, when a student with whom he had cared enough to establish a personal relationship committed suicide.

As I developed a teaching style that reflected the opposite of his words, I found the satisfaction and joy that only comes from helping students become their own heroes. I often wondered how many of the three hundred teachers-in-training in that classroom took the professor's advice and missed that joy. If teachers do not care enough to become involved with their students in any way except in relation to their subject matter, becoming one's own hero is not only impossible with the teacher, but is frustrated within the students. Education that does not stop at the neck but is integrated into the whole person allows both students and teachers to become their own heroes.

Self-Help Books

Unable to find help in facilitating becoming their own heroes through formal education, many people turn to self-help books. There are certainly numerous wonderful and helpful books available, but they must be chosen and read with a very selective eye.

Authors can have a powerful influence in either facilitating or frustrating becoming your own hero. It is easy to be seduced by the authority of authors who, like most authorities, often thrive on hooking your belief that they have whatever answer you are seeking. If you are seeking help fixing your car or cooking a delicious meal, you certainly want to get the factual information that best comes from an expert. But entrusting your mind to someone else is a far weightier decision.

Implicit in most self-help books is the promise of an expert who claims not only to have the answers for which you are looking, but also to have a simple formula for achieving that end. Following these dictates must, in the long run, prove to be very unsatisfying.

For example, books relating to weight loss that give diets or simplistic ideas not only do not work in the long term, but also subtly undermine what little self-confidence was there in the first place. When it is implied that something is easy to do and you do not accomplish it, you are naturally left with self-doubt. Failing to accomplish what has been implied as simple leaves us with the question "What's wrong with me?"

Geneen Roth, author of such books as *Appetites, Breaking Free From Compulsive Eating,* and *When Food Is Love,* is one of those rare writers on weight and eating problems whose writing helps facilitate becoming your own hero. She helps her readers gain self-respect and self-trust by going to the core of the problem and unveiling ideas that will help resolve food and eating issues. It is not always easy, but it is real and long-lasting.

Then there are the books that give simplistic ideas for making your relationships better. Simplistic answers to complex problems, like "Men are . . ." and "What women want is . . ." usually do little to improve your ability to create Fulfilling Connections. They may serve to harden stereotypes, further Disconnecting Beliefs, and make it harder to feel compassion for yourself and others.

John Welwood, in *Love and Awakening*, presents his ideas without any pretense of an easy fix or divine guidance. The following is an example of how he shares well-grounded ideas to help open your heart to yourself and others: "If falling in love provides a glimpse of our true nature, entering into a long-term relationship brings us up against all the obstacles to residing here—whatever prevents us from being present, being real, being ourselves. I don't know any couples who have not suffered this fall from grace at some point, losing touch with the original bright presence that first drew them together. Yet this is not a problem when we understand it as an integral part of a couple's journey toward greater wholeness and a richer, more seasoned kind of love."

The Guru Papers is an example of a book that uncovers the difficulties that occur from living under the constant barrage of authoritarian dictates that disconnect you from your compassion. The following quote from the preface of *The Guru Papers* reflects how the authors maintain their humility and yet powerfully state their message:

"We feel strongly about the point of view presented in this book, in part because it has helped explain for us why things are the way they are, and also why they must change. We present our perspective as clearly, forcefully, and accurately as we know how. Consequently, some might find the tone of this book uncompromising—perhaps to the extent of wondering if it is itself authoritarian. To this we can only respond that we have spent many years examining these issues, including what others have thought. To date we have not found a more inclusive perspective, and thus have a surety and confidence in what we are saying. But confidence need not be authoritarian in itself if one is truly open to being shown wrong. The essence of ideological authoritarianism is unchallengeability, not confidence. This book presents our current viewpoint, which in our own minds is subject to revision, structural changes, and even being abandoned, should we or others find telling weaknesses."

That brings us to yours truly. I hope *Becoming Your Own Hero* has been a challenging, supportive, and useful experience. I have tried to present my ideas simply, but not simplistically. I make no claims that they are "the truth" and no promises for your attempts to implement them. They are merely the best expression of what I have found to be true in my struggle to overcome my Disconnecting Beliefs and learn to live with my Heart Feelings and find more Fulfilling Connections and become more of my own hero. My ideas will continue to change and deepen as I change and deepen. If they resonate for you and help you to make more sense and get greater joy out of this gift of life we have been given, I am happy.

Appendix

The Fulfilling Connections Process:
Seven Steps to Becoming Your Own Hero

The Fulfilling Connections Process (FCP) is a seven-step process designed to help you make Fulfilling Connections the focus of everything you do, learn how to increase the moments you experience them, practically integrate Heart Feelings into your everyday life, and be your own hero more of the time. The FCP can be used over and over again in every area of your life and result in any activity becoming more satisfying.

The seven steps are listed below, followed by a detailed explanation of each step. At the end of the appendix is a completed sample form, followed by a blank form that can be reproduced for your future use.

1. Describe a situation/activity about which you are feeling unhappy, frustrated, and/or dissatisfied.
2. Write a goal statement describing your desire for Fulfilling Connections and what it means to be connected to your Heart Feelings.
3. Write a commitment to Heart Learning statement.
4. Describe the disconnected/unloving feelings and behaviors toward yourself and others that are present in the situation and the results.
5. Envision how you would behave and what would result if your Heart Feelings were operational and you were nurturing the Heart Feelings of others.
6. List the fears and beliefs disconnecting you from your Heart Feelings and the purpose they are serving.
7. Design a plan for moving toward overcoming your disconnecting fears and beliefs.

A Detailed Explanation of Each Step

Step 1—Describe a situation/activity about which you are feeling unhappy, frustrated, and/or dissatisfied.

The FCP is rooted in the idea that difficulties or unhappiness are valuable opportunities for learning to increase the moments of being your own hero and open the door for Fulfilling Connections with others. Any unresolved problem can be used. It could be related to another person or a situation in your life. For example:

- Your child is not doing well in school, spending too much time in front of the TV, seeming withdrawn and noncommunicative, not doing homework, going to bed too late, not being responsible.
- Your spouse with whom you are having difficulties, such as: not wanting to make love as often as you do or in ways you would like, not keeping the house as neat as you would like, habitually being late, not being truthful, having an affair, not sharing thoughts or feelings, not sharing your interests in certain activities, treating money in ways you don't like, being unhappy about how you talk or don't talk about difficult issues, worrying about his or her use of drugs.
- Your boss, who is too demanding, doesn't treat you fairly and/or respectfully.
- You are unhappy with yourself over weight or eating habits, lack of motivation, excessive spending, boredom, general dissatisfaction with life, depression.

The situation you choose to address is relatively unimportant because within almost every situation are the lessons that apply to almost all other situations. For example, within difficulties related to spending money, in addition to your beliefs and fears about abundance or scarcity, are how you react when things don't go your way (control or avoidance) and the power struggles within yourself and with others that result. These beliefs, fears and reactions infect many other situations and are at the core of most unhappiness.

Step 2—Write a goal statement describing your desire for Fulfilling Connections and what it means to be connected to your Heart Feelings.

Like any effective process, it is important to begin at the end by knowing where you want to go. However, this goal statement differs significantly from typical goal-setting practices because *the goal is not an outcome, but a state of being.*

When you are convinced that Fulfilling Connections are what you need to feel truly fulfilled, setting it as your goal will have a powerful effect on your behavior. It is the absence of that awareness that leaves people adrift pursuing things, rather than directed toward a way of being that will satisfy them.

To begin with the end in mind, it is very helpful to have a picture of what your goal will look like. In terms of the FCP, that picture is how you would see yourself when connected to your Heart Feelings and being your own hero. Picturing a state of being differs significantly from those programs that ask you to imagine an outcome you wish to bring about. Such ideas merely support the mistaken belief that you can have control over others and/or things. Imagining a state of being, on the other hand, requires the faith that a connection to your Heart Feelings will bring about satisfying results.

To get a sense of what it means to be connected to your heart, remember a time when you saw deeply into another person, a time when you sensed another person's perfection so that they became both physically and emotionally beautiful. At such a time, you saw behind this person's fears and protective behavior and into their soul. Compassion filled your heart and you saw that they were doing the best they could and that they were lovable. You truly appreciated them and it was probably an awesome and memorable experience. Such an experience of unconditional love is characteristic of being connected to your Heart Feelings.

Although picturing an outcome is not part of the FCP, you will probably find yourself indulging in the very human tendency of wanting to sneak in an outcome from time to time. For example, you might imagine an outcome in which the two of you feel close, are laughing and having a good time, or are making love; or you may envision the other person becoming aware that his behavior is hurting himself and others and that he needs to learn more about himself, or his seeing the essence of you and valuing that essence. This will not get in the way of Fulfilling Connections *as long as you maintain the outcome as a possibility and do not become attached to it.*

Your goal statement is written each time that you begin the FCP as a constant reminder of your intent. As your understanding of Fulfilling Connections deepens you may wish to amend it.

The following is an example of a Fulfilling Connections goal statement:

I want to stay connected to my Heart Feelings and to those of others as much as I can. I want to be open and accepting of whatever feelings and situations come up within me and others, maintaining my compassion and faith that this process will lead me toward discovering the best solution for this problem.

Step 3—Write a commitment to Heart Learning statement.

A commitment to a Heart Learning statement describes your understanding of what it means to maintain an openness to learning and to create a safe environment for that learning to occur. It is asked for each time that you begin the FCP to help maintain a focus on your commitment.

It is important that you begin the FCP only when you believe that you are open to learning. But also remember that even when you welcome new self-knowledge, there will be times during the process when you may close to learning. When this occurs, give yourself time to explore your feelings and to understand why this has happened. Think about what you may have discovered about yourself that was frightening or challenging. Once you resolve whatever is blocking your openness, you can begin the FCP again.

Alternating periods of being open and closed may occur at any time. When you are closed to learning, the first step in opening again is acknowledging that you are closed. By simply asking yourself, "Am I open to learning?" or "Is my heart open?" you may be shocked how many times the answer is "No."

The statement you write today will change as your understanding increases of what learning entails. As with your goal statement, you may wish to amend it in the future. The following is an example of a Heart Learning statement:

Learning, especially about myself, is my birthright and it determines my destiny. I am determined to confront the unflattering, unacknowledged, or unpleasant aspects of myself. I realize that I must create a safe learning environment if I am to accomplish that. I will falter and close myself off to learning at times, but with determination and help I will open again and continue my journey.

Step 4—Describe the disconnected/unloving feelings and behaviors toward yourself and others that are present in the situation and the results.

This step asks you to list the behaviors that have been disconnected/unloving, and connect them to the negative results you are experiencing.

Your disconnected/unloving behaviors may have been your initial reactions to what another person did for themselves, to you, or to themselves. The following sampling of answers to Step 4 might have occurred if the characters from some of the examples in this book's teaching stories had used the FCP:

Reaction to someone doing something for themselves:
Bill reacting to getting the bills for Mary's gift giving, from Chapter Five—

"I tried to get her to see where she was irresponsible. I was irritated but thought I hid it pretty well. She was apologetic but I wound up feeling awful. I'm beginning to think that some things, like her rebellion and our lack of closeness, may be related. I'll have to ask her about this."

George reacting to Marie telling him about her outing with Troy, from Chapter Four—

"I was pissed off with Marie and called her names. She snapped back, put me down for being so uptight, and we were off to the races. I hate our arguments and really feel bad about myself when I am disrespectful toward her."

Reaction to someone doing something disconnected/unloving toward you:
Mary reacting to Bill lecturing her, from Chapter Five—

"I tried making him happy even though I really didn't think there was anything wrong with my behavior. Whether I do that, or agree with him and later do what I want with a 'fuck you' attitude, I wind up feeling bad about myself and don't feel very close with him."

Marie reacting to George's criticism, from Chapter Four—

"George tried to control me and I bristled and got really pissy. Sometimes I control that urge and write him letters telling him about his disrespectful behavior. But either way I feel lousy. I'm feeling more and more distant from him and closer to Troy."

Reaction to someone doing something disconnected/unloving to themselves:
Parent, reacting to child's use of marijuana, from Chapter Six—

"I got angry. I also lectured him, gave him advice, and threatened to punish him. He closed up and has not spoken to me since. I feel bad that I hurt him and I feel alone."

Shawna reacting to her mother's depression, from Chapter Two—

"I blamed myself for Mom's depression and, feeling responsible for her well-being, committed myself to never doing anything that would upset her. I feel dead inside and the only pleasure I get comes from eating, especially sweets."

If the situation does not involve another person, write everything you can think of that has not shown compassion for yourself and the results.

Examples:

Unhappiness with one's job—
"I'm miserable at work. I'm bored most of the time and I'm drinking and getting stoned more of the time. I feel like such a jerk and a loser. I find myself being very critical of myself and I'm feeling more and more depressed.

Unhappiness with weight and not sticking to diet—
"I get really upset with myself for not following through on my commitments. I feel like I'm my father trying to motivate me with either pep talks or put downs, like calling myself a quitter and telling myself that I'll never amount to anything unless I just do it."

The following exercise may be helpful in answering Step 4:

1. Sit back, relax, and take some deep breaths. Close your eyes and replay the situation.
2. Remember how you looked and the feelings that were in your body.
3. Picture the other person's response and imagine what was going on in his or her body.
4. Remember what went on between the two of you and how you felt when the interaction ended, an hour later, and the next day.

To discover more of your disconnected/unloving behaviors, it may be helpful to review the lists of disconnected/unloving feelings and behaviors and their results that follow. You can return to them whenever you are using the FCP.

Disconnected Feelings

As you go through this list, if you have difficulty identifying a feeling as disconnected, put it through the test of whether compassion was predominant and whether an intent to learn was present.

Anger	Selfishness	Arrogance
Guilt	Hopelessness	Revenge
Hatred	Vengeance	Jealousy
Excesssive anxiety	Sadness as a victim ("poor me")	

Disconnected Behaviors

As you go through this list, it will help to give you dignity and respect by remembering that your intent, usually unconscious, was to cover up vulnerable feelings and thus protect yourself.

- Telling feelings with a hidden agenda; for example, to get another to change their behavior
- Threats
- Actually carrying out the threats
- Lecturing
- Judgmental criticism including calling names like stupid, jerk, ass hole, idiot
- Giving advice
- Withdrawing into indifference—giving up
- Withdrawing into angry silence (withdrawing love)
- Crying as a victim (poor me)
- Caretaking (regularly doing for others what they are capable of doing for themselves)

Results of disconnected feelings and behaviors

Loneliness	Emptiness	Fighting	Eroded self-esteem
Resistance	Power struggles	Fear	Eroded love
Deadness	Distance	Boredom	

Step 5—Envision how you would behave and what would result if your Heart Feelings were operational and you were nurturing the Heart Feelings of others.

Finding the Heart Feelings and behavior that will nurture yourself and others is often not easy. It is the behavior that occurs naturally when compassion dominates over fear, and you feel self-confident in the faith that, no matter what happens, you will thrive.

These moments are rare, especially when others are behaving in ways that are potentially threatening to you and/or to them. In movies being one's own hero is depicted in those infrequent scenes when people open their hearts to themselves and others. Romantic music fills the theater and you are likely to feel emotionally touched.

Behaviors that come from Heart Feelings are neither knee-jerk reactions, nor the same every time. Rather, they are creative and compassionate responses uniquely appropriate to you, the other person, and the situation. The answers that follow continue from the examples in Step 4 as if characters from the book had used the FCP.

Responses to someone doing something for themselves:
Bill responding to getting the bills for Mary's gift giving–

"I would be open to learning about her thoughts and feelings, especially those related to her ideas about gift giving and money and which, if any, of her responses are related to things that are going on between us. I'm sure she would like that. I think I would feel really good about myself and we would be more intimate."

George responding to Marie telling him about her outing with Troy–

"I would be genuinely happy that she was happy and would want to share her excitement with her. If I become upset by what she is doing, I would want to find out what is blocking my openness. That would feel great and we would be much closer."

Responses to someone doing something disconnected/unloving towards you:
Mary responding to Bill lecturing her–

"I would tell Bill that it feels awful when he is condescending. I would want to understand the very good reasons why I am afraid of being up-front with him. When his heart was open, I would ask for his help in gaining a better understanding of my fears. That would leave me feeling very powerful."

Marie responding to George's criticism–

"If I didn't take George's upset personally, I would realize that he's scared and, remembering that he is having a difficult time, I would stay open to hearing his feelings even if they were blaming me. I think I would really like myself responding that way, but I'm not sure how he would respond."

Responses to someone doing something disconnected/unloving to themselves:
Parent, responding to child's use of marijuana–

"I would express my concern, my fears for his safety, and try to create a safe atmosphere for us to be able to talk more honestly. I would ask him what I was doing that was making it difficult for him to be open with me. That would be an honest reaction and would feel great."

Shawna responding to her mother's depression–

"I would maintain my caring for my mother, but not hold myself back from doing what truly nurtures me. I'm not real sure how that would look, but I know it isn't indulging in sweets. I must begin finding out what it means to be loving to myself."

For responses to situations that do not involve another person, write everything you can that shows compassion for yourself.

Examples:

Unhappiness with one's job–

"Maybe if I could find out what's got me stuck, I could get unstuck. I want to set a course to discover what kind of work will excite me and what's keeping me back from going for it. If I could be working toward a better situation, I would feel really good about myself and this situation would be much more tolerable."

Unhappiness with weight and not sticking to diet–

"When I realize that there are good reasons for my behavior I would stop trying to make myself change. Not putting myself down would feel like a breath of fresh air. It would probably open the space for something different to occur."

It may be helpful in finding the behavior that accompanies Heart Feelings to try remembering and identifying with the person you most associate with openhearted acceptance and imagining how that person would respond in this situation. Many people might serve as your model, including a parent, relative, teacher, neighbor, historical figure, or even a character from a movie.

For example, the person in my life who best embodied a loving openness was my grandfather. My father was both physically and emotionally absent most of the time, but Grandpa Barney took me on long walks in the park and to baseball games where we shared a lot more than just hot dogs and merry-go-round rides. Every Friday evening he brought home a new book, and we had our special time reading and talking together.

Grandpa was a romantic, a poet and lover with a soft face and a warm heart. An immigrant tailor who never got caught up in the American dream, his easygoing ways were the subject of much ridicule from other family members who were better taskmasters. But Grandpa was the only person in my youth who demonstrated a connection to the emotional and compassionate part of ourselves. I didn't really appreciate this until, as an adult looking to recover hidden parts of myself, I remembered the one male person who was brave enough not to deny the loving aspects of his humanness.

I have also gotten ideas for finding the behavior that accompanies Heart Feelings from books and films. For example, upon reading *Open Mind, Open Heart* by Thomas Keating, I was very touched by his description of contemplative prayer.

I began practicing this meditation, which asks you to focus on something that represents love. I chose to meditate on light. I had been meditating on light for about a month when, during one session, a figure began appearing in the light. As it came more into focus, I recognized it to be Jesus.

I was shocked. I thought to myself, "What are you doing in my meditation, I'm not even Christian? In fact, my grandfather was a rabbi and if he knew you were here, I don't think he would be too pleased."

Not having much personal knowledge of Jesus, I began reading everything I could about Jesus the person, the "pre-Easter Jesus." I became fascinated with this person and he soon became a model for how to respond with Heart Feelings, regardless of the situation. When I was in difficult situations, I began asking myself, "How would Jesus respond?" The results were fantastic.

I began searching for both women and men, real or fictional, to serve as role models to help me stay connected to both my strength and my love. I haven't found many models, but when I do I bring that person into my meditation and imagine him or her as my guardian angel, there to help me learn to become more of the person I want to be.

Creating a meditation to open your heart might also facilitate finding your answers. The following meditation has been very helpful for me:

1. Breathe deeply and visualize how you would look and feel as a secure, open, and loving person.
2. Call into your consciousness times when you connected to the best place inside of you.
3. Recall times when you felt content and proud of who you were, with nothing to hide and nothing to prove. Such experiences may have occurred in nature or during your everyday activities. Remembering those times will confirm that you are capable of opening your heart.

Information to help you answer this oftentimes perplexing step might be found in the "Becoming Your Own Hero, Fulfilling Connections and Possibilities" section in each of the teaching stories. Once you discover the compassionate response, if you find yourself unable to do it, the place to look for what's blocking that response is your fears and beliefs.

Step 6—List the fears and beliefs disconnecting you from your Heart Feelings and the purpose they are serving.
Identifying Disconnecting Beliefs and understanding the impact they are having will deepen the more you use the FCP. The biggest challenge involves facing your disconnecting beliefs and behaviors and the resulting pain and fear they have caused you and others. When these beliefs dominate your life, you are cut off from your compassionate self, those you love, and from a sense of spiritual presence.

The following responses are a continuation of the journey begun in Steps 4 and 5 of characters and situations from the book.

Reaction to someone doing something for themselves:
Bill regarding Mary's gift giving–

"I'm afraid that if I am accepting I will not have control over Mary and she will spend frivolously. I'm afraid of my own freedom as well. I must look at my beliefs about freedom and faith."

George regarding Marie telling him about her outing with Troy–

"I'm afraid that I'm not adequate in many areas and I need to have control over Marie. If I lose her I'll be lost. I need to look at the beliefs about my limitations and my beliefs about being alone."

Responding to someone doing something disconnected/unloving towards you:
Mary regarding Bill lecturing her–

"I'm afraid I can't take care of myself financially and believe I deserve to be treated disrespectfully when I misbehave. I need to look at my beliefs about my limitations and my right not to be treated disrespectfully no matter what I do."

Marie regarding George's criticism—
"I don't believe I have the right to do what I want if it upsets my lover and therefore I don't believe I can take good care of myself. I need to look at my beliefs about caretaking."

Responding to someone doing something disconnected/unloving to themselves:
Parent, regarding child's use of marijuana—
"I'm terrified of my child having the freedom to experiment and find his own way in life. I don't have faith in him and I guess I don't have faith in myself. I need to look at my fears about not being in control and my beliefs about my limitations and about death."

Shawna regarding her mother's depression—
"I'm so afraid of upsetting people because I believe their upsets are my fault. This is a major reason why I can't let go and be spontaneous. I need to explore the beliefs surrounding my fears and beliefs around upsetting other people."

If the situation does not involve another person, write everything that fuels your doubts and perpetuates your disconnected/unloving behavior.

Examples:

Unhappiness with one's job—
"I don't think there's anything special about me and even if there was I would be afraid to follow my passion. I need to look at my beliefs about my lack of worth."

Unhappiness with weight and not sticking to diet—
"I believe that the way to get myself to behave is to keep nagging myself and flagellating myself to get the job done. I guess I don't have faith in myself, that I know what's best for me. I need to look at the beliefs that erode my self-esteem.

Step 7—Design a plan for moving toward overcoming your disconnecting fears and beliefs.

As stated in Chapter Eight, there is no single right road for your journey. The challenge will be finding the one(s) that best serve you. Remember that each of the characters in the stories found different paths that suited them. All were both therapeutic and spiritual, but not all were formal therapy or traditional religion.

The only consistent criterion on which you need to stay focused is whether you are finding the courage to respond more of the time with Heart Feelings. Such openness will create more Fulfilling Connections and will be reflected in your sense of well-being increasing and the quality of the relationships. Evaluating your experiences through the filter of whether or not they encourage connection to your Heart Feelings will significantly affect your choice of lovers, friends, activities, and ways of reacting to things you do not like or that upset you.

The two exercises that follow might be helpful and can be part of your plan.

Exercise 1: **Recognizing how rigidly held beliefs affect your life**

1. Write a belief you hold for which there is no universal agreement or factual proof that it is the truth.
2. Do you really believe it to be an incontrovertible fact? If your answer is yes, go directly to #5. If your answer is no, go to #3.
3. Do other people think you believe it is a fact? (You can check it out by asking friends and family.)
4. If a preponderance of people believe you believe it, you can learn about the things you may be doing that give your utterances such definitiveness. If people give you authority and power, ask them about your part in creating a system that disempowers them and blocks fulfilling connections. Ask them about your body language (facial expressions, tightness in your arms and torso), tone of voice, and defensiveness. Become more introspective and aware of any internal tension and hardness that may close off your learning.
5. What are the results of holding a belief rigidly with people who do not believe as you do? How do people react–for example, argumentatively, compliantly, or judgmentally? How do you feel about the lack of Heart Learning discussions and Fulfilling Connections that result?

6. What do you fear happening if you held a belief as a personal truth and a choice rather than as a fact? As examples, you may fear being mistaken and unlovable, out of control, left adrift, rejected, or lonely. Or, you may fear that you might be unable to maintain the belief because it would not have authority, and that just believing it because it feels good, and you like it, may not be enough. If that is so, what might happen then?

Exercise #2—**Overcoming Disconnecting Beliefs**

Once you have discovered a Disconnecting Belief, the following are possibilities for working with it:

1. Explore how you got the belief and why you adopted it.

See if you can figure out where the belief came from. Did you hear it from one of your close relatives and decide that it was the right way to be? Was it taught to you in your religious training or by your peers? Did you get it through books you read or from television programs?

2. Explore what purpose the belief is now serving.

Discovering the source of your beliefs may be interesting, but it is just a starting point. Much more important is to realize how the belief serves you today. One way to approach this is by asking what you fear happening if you were to let go of the belief. Protecting yourself from what you fear is how the belief is serving you.

Think of the many beliefs you adopted in childhood that have disappeared. When a belief does not serve some important purpose, we automatically let it go. For example, we may have been taught that sex before marriage is wrong. If we still believe that, then either abstaining from premarital sex, or else engaging in it and feeling guilty about it, continues to serve us in some way.

3. Prepare yourself for testing out the belief, especially by practicing self-acceptance.

Preparing to test out beliefs requires strengthening both your self-esteem and support system. Very few people ever jump into difficult water without developing their ability to swim and making sure that there are people around to help them should they get into trouble.

Perhaps the most important preparation is opening your heart to yourself and respecting wherever you are in the exploration process. This means learning to not make yourself wrong during those times when you are disconnected from your Heart Feelings and accepting that, in those moments, protecting yourself and not testing out your beliefs is more important than having a Fulfilling Connection.

4. Test out your disconnecting beliefs and explore how you are holding them. You got a glimpse of a portion my own journey in Chapter Three as I confronted some of my demons on the way toward more Fulfilling Connections. Your journey will take its own unique shape.

The Fulfilling Connections Process—
Sample Form

1. Describe a situation/activity about which you are feeling unhappy, frustrated, and/or dissatisfied.

I expected Ellen home at 10 and she didn't arrive until after midnight.

2. Write a goal statement describing your desire for Fulfilling Connections and what it means to be connected to your Heart Feelings.

I know that Fulfilling Connections are what will satisfy me and I want more of them. When my heart is open I will be soft, available, and open to learning.

3. Write a commitment to Heart Learning statement.

Learning about how I can be a more loving person and how to create a safe environment for my own learning and that of others is very important to me. I know I must be willing to look at some things about myself that will be scary and I am willing to seek help in getting there.

4. Describe the disconnected/unloving feelings and behaviors toward yourself and others that are present in the situation and the results.

I blew up, was critical, and tried to induce guilt. I got a defensive tirade back. We patched things up, but I still feel hurt and there's a palpable distance between us.

5. Envision how you would behave and what would result if your Heart Feelings were operational and you were nurturing the Heart Feelings of others.

I would tell her I love her and I was so afraid she was hurt or worse and that I feel so relieved that she is okay. I would remember that there are very good reasons why she didn't call and want to explore why that didn't happen. She would feel cared about and loved and that would make me feel wonderful.

6. List the fears and beliefs disconnecting you from Heart Feelings and the purpose they are serving.

I believe my anger will make her behave differently. I'm afraid that if I don't have control, bad things will happen and worrying keeps them from happening. I need to look at my beliefs about faith and life.

7. Design a plan for moving toward overcoming your disconnecting fears and beliefs.

I will talk with some of my friends to see what has helped them in becoming more loving. I hope to get some suggestions of books to read, and perhaps there is a group I could join that might help me. In the meantime I will work with the Process for Overcoming Disconnecting Beliefs.

The Fulfilling Connections Process

1. Describe a situation/activity about which you are feeling unhappy, frustrated and/or dissatisfied.

2. Write a goal statement describing your desire for Fulfilling Connections and what it means to be connected to your Heart Feelings.

3. Write a commitment to Heart Learning statement.

4. Describe the disconnected/unloving feelings and behaviors toward yourself and others that are present in the situation and the results.

5. Envision how you would behave and what would result if your Heart Feelings were operational and you were nurturing the Heart Feelings of others.

6. List the fears and beliefs disconnecting you from Heart Feelings and the purpose they are serving.

7. Design a plan for moving toward overcoming your disconnecting fears and beliefs.

About The Author

After reading this book you probably already know more about me than you wanted, or needed, to know. But, there's a little more I would like you to know. In 1989, I said I did not want to practice psychotherapy any longer and since then I have been very happy providing, when asked, emotional help to my friends. This has proved very satisfying for me (and I hope for them). I have learned a lot during this process and would like to offer my services again, but in a very different way and on a very limited basis. I am available for Fulfillment Coaching and you can find out about this at my web site: www.DrJordanPaul.com.. There's a whole lot more information on the site about my various books, being of service, conflict resolution, and my speaking and workshop schedule. There is probably more than you want to know, but I hope you'll check it out anyway.

Order Form

QTY.	Title	Price	Can. Price	Total
	Becoming Your Own Hero **Dr. Paul Jordan**	$16.95	$22.95	
	Shipping and Handling Add $4.95 for orders in the US			
	Sales tax (WA state residents only, add 8.9%			
	Total enclosed			

Telephone Orders:
Call 1-800-461-1931
Have your Visa or
MasterCard ready.

INTL. Telephone Orders:
Toll free 1-877-250-5500
Have your credit card ready.

Fax Order:
425-398-1380
Fill out this form and fax.

Postal Orders:
Hara Publishing
P.O. Box 19732
Seattle, WA 98109

E-mail Orders:
harapub@foxinternet.net

Method of Payment:

☐   Check or Money Order

☐   VISA

☐   MasterCard

_____
Card#

_____
Expiration Date

_____
Signature

Name_____

Address_____

City_____**State**_____**Zip**_____

Phone (**)** _____**Fax**_____

Quantity discounts are available.
Call 425-398-3679 for more information.
Thank you for your order!